Perspectives in American History

No. 2
THE FRENCH IN THE MISSISSIPPI VALLEY, 1740-1750

THE FRENCH
IN THE MISSISSIPPI VALLEY
1740-1750

BY

NORMAN WARD CALDWELL

PORCUPINE PRESS
Philadelphia 1974

Library of Congress Cataloging in Publication Data

Caldwell, Norman Ward, 1905-1958.
　The French in the Mississippi Valley, 1740-1750.

　(Perspectives in American history, no. 2)
　Reprint of the 1941 ed. published by the University of Illinois Press, Urbana, which was issued as v. 26, no. 3 of Illinois studies in the social sciences.
　Bibliography: p.
　1. Mississippi Valley--History--To 1803.
2. French in the Mississippi Valley. 3. France--Colonies--North America. I. Title. II. Series: Perspectives in American history (Philadelphia) no. 2. III. Series: Illinois. University. Illinois studies in the social sciences, v. 26, no. 3.
F352.C33　1974　　　　　977'.01　　　　73-18443
ISBN 0-87991-330-4

First edition 1941
(Urbana: *Illinois Studies in the Social Sciences,*
vol. xxvi, no. 3, 1941)

Reprinted 1974 by
PORCUPINE PRESS, INC.
1317 Filbert St.
Philadelphia, Pennsylvania 19107

Manufactured in the United States of America

PREFACE

THE DECADE 1740-1750 was one of supreme importance to the future of the French colonies in North America. It was in this period that war was resumed between England and France after a generation of peace. Though the struggle between the two great powers for the hegemony of North America was thus resumed, four years of fighting (1744-1748) resulted only in the re-establishment of the *status quo ante bellum*. The peace of Aix-la-Chapelle, then, merely called a temporary halt to the general struggle, and both sides began at once to prepare for the early reopening of hostilities.

It has constantly been the purpose of the writer to make a detailed study of this period with the view of determining the importance of the of the western regions in shaping the destiny of French power in America. Though secondary works have been carefully consulted, the study as presented is based almost entirely on source materials, many of which are now used for the first time. In the French documents, the expense accounts for the western posts (*Archives Nationales,* Series C^{11}A) have been searched carefully. This material, which has been consistently overlooked by scholars in the past, has given a wealth of detailed information on the political, social, and economic life of the times. Likewise the *Vaudreuil Manuscripts,* now used for the first time, have revealed important information on affairs in southern Louisiana. The use of the colonial records of South Carolina and Georgia as found in the *Public Record Office* has shed new light on the southeastern border region in this period.

This study was begun in 1935-1936 as a doctoral dissertation. At that time the writer limited the subject to the "upper country"—the *pays d'en haut* of the French. Additional research in 1938 and later has led to a broadening of the scope of the study so as to include more of affairs in the southern part of the country. For example, the pursuit of the roots of the Chickasaw problem has emphasized Franco-English relations in the southeastern region.

In the first chapter of this study, the governmental system of New France is described in order to introduce the reader to the nature of the colonial administration, the various problems presented, and the weaknesses inherent. Then follows a chapter on the population and industry of the western country, emphasizing the difficulties of settlement, the crude conditions of culture and industry, and the plans proposed for development. In the third chapter the fur trade is treated with particular reference to the western country. Here an attempt is made to give fullest details of the Anglo-French commercial rivalry and its bearing on political conditions. Lack of space has necessitated the omission of one important phase of the subject of trade expansion in this period, namely, the story of the La Vérendryes and the extension of French power and trade into the country to the west of Lake Superior. Next, problems related to Indian affairs are discussed in detail, first in reference to the region about the Great Lakes and the activities of western Indians in King George's War, and then in reference to the Chickasaw problem in the south. The important subject of Anglo-French rivalry in the south during this period is summarized briefly, this having been treated fully in an article published elsewhere. Finally, the Indian uprising in the western country in 1747 is discussed with particular reference to consequent problems arising from the English penetration into the Ohio valley. The accompanying map is designed to familiarize the reader with place names, routes of travel, location of Indian tribes, etc. A selected bibliography is added which lists the most suitable materials on the period, without, however, making any claim to being exhaustive.

The indebtedness of the writer to those who have assisted in the preparation of this study is very great. Special acknowledgment is due to Professor T. C. Pease of the University of Illinois, who first suggested the subject and who made many suggestions and criticisms which have been very helpful. Professor F. C. Dietz, also of the University of Illinois, has been very kind in offering suggestions from time to time. Acknowledgment is also due to the librarians and staff members of the following libraries for their cooperation and fine spirit of helpfulness in making materials available: the Illinois Historical Survey, Urbana; the University of Illinois Library, Urbana; the Libraries of the University of Chicago; the Newberry Library, Chicago; and the Library of Congress, Washington, D. C. Nor would I forget Miss Marjorie Lee Cox, Miss Aileen Byrn, Miss Frances Smith, and others of the College of the Ozarks, along with my wife, Mrs. Amy Caldwell, all of whom have labored faithfully at those tasks incident to the preparation of the manuscript. The writer is alone responsible for all opinions expressed.

CONTENTS

I. Political and Financial Administration of New France ... 9

II. Population and Industry ... 35

III. The Fur Trade ... 51

IV. General Indian Relations ... 64

V. The Indian Uprising of 1747 and the Ohio Question ... 86

Summary and Conclusions ... 101

Bibliography ... 103

Index ... 111

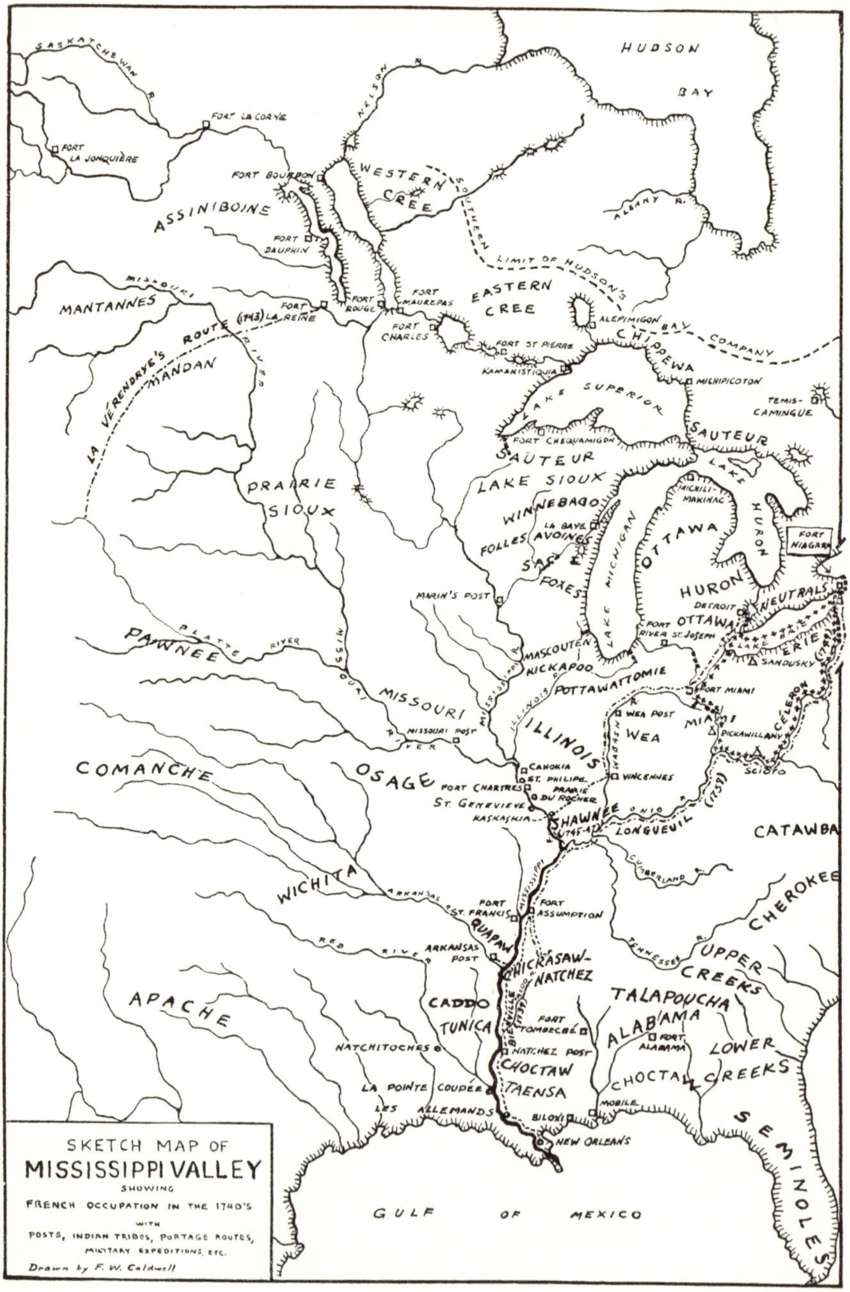

SKETCH MAP OF
MISSISSIPPI VALLEY
SHOWING
FRENCH OCCUPATION IN THE 1740'S
WITH
POSTS, INDIAN TRIBES, PORTAGE ROUTES, MILITARY EXPEDITIONS, ETC.
Drawn by F. W. Caldwell

CHAPTER I

POLITICAL AND FINANCIAL ADMINISTRATION OF NEW FRANCE

THE FRENCH COLONIES in America were governed from France through the Department of the Marine under the immediate control of the Minister of the Marine. This minister as a member of the Council of State was directly responsible to the king. In general, the plan was to govern Canada and Louisiana as if they were provinces of France. The two colonies were governed separately, but the fact that Canada was much older than Louisiana and much more populous meant that Louisiana was somewhat dependent on Canada.[1]

Over each colony was placed a governor, appointed by the king, and another official of equal rank, called the intendant, who shared with the governor the management of the colony. The governor was usually a naval officer, and he was nominally in charge of the defense and general administration of the colony. He served at the pleasure of the king, and when relieved generally went back into the active service of the navy. His office was the same in Canada as in Louisiana. In Canada, however, he is more often designated by the appellation of *general* instead of *governor*. His salary in Canada, including his perquisites, amounted to about 20,000 livres, while in Louisiana he received considerably less.[2] The Canadian governor commonly resided at Quebec, while New Orleans was the home of the governor of Louisiana. When the governor travelled into any part of his colony, his power superseded that of the local authorities (the sub-governors). In other words, his power went with him as the king's court followed the king in medieval England.

The *intendant* shared with the governor the colonial administration. He was charged with independent jurisdiction over the police, finances, and justice of the colony, and he had an appeal to the minister in case of friction with the governor. The two officials served as checks upon each other, this being a contrivance to secure efficient administration in an autocratic and centralized system of government. Like the governor, the intendant was appointed by the king and served at his pleasure. His salary in Canada with his perquisites amounted to some 16,000 livres per year, while in Louisiana it was about 8,000 livres.[3] In Canada both governor and intendant spent much of their time at Montreal on various

---

[1]For example, the Canadian governor had control over licenses for the trade in the Illinois country. Louisiana, being comparatively weaker in military power, was also dependent on Canada in time of war, sometimes requesting Canadian troops for assistance. Then, too, in regard to Indian policy, the Canadian governor exerted a wide control at times.
[2]*Bordereau*, 1741, *Archives Nationales, Colonies*, C¹¹A, 114:381ᵛ. The Louisiana governor received 12,000 livres according to the *Bordereau* of 1745. *Ibid.*, C¹³A, 29:237-238.
[3]Canada, *Bordereau*, 1741, *Ibid.*, C¹¹A, 114:381ᵛ; Louisiana, *Bordereau*, 1745, *Ibid.*, C¹³A, 29:237-238.

business. When the intendant was absent from the country, or incapacitated, the deputy intendant at Montreal succeeded him.[4] The intendant necessarily relied on his deputies for the discharge of many of his duties, especially in the case of expenditures, which were very largely made at Montreal.[5]

Under such a system we would expect friction to arise between the governor and intendant concerning the scope of their powers. From time to time the minister had to determine questions of that nature, such as the instance in 1746, when a controversy arose over which official had the exclusive right to issue orders to the officers of the king's ships. The minister ruled that this was the power of the governor alone, though it was expected that he would consult his colleague.[6] Since the intendant controlled expenditures, friction often developed over such subjects as expense accounts when "moderated" by the intendant and also over issues from the king's stores.[7]

An outstanding example of friction between these two officials is found in the case involving the judicial powers of the intendant relative to the western posts. This controversy grew out of a suit brought by M. de Lorme, a Montreal merchant, against M. Dailleboust, another merchant of that city, to restrain Dailleboust from collecting a debt owed him by the Sieur de la Vérendrye, who was exploiting the trading posts in the far northwest. De Lorme pleaded that, having himself a debt of priority with M. de la Vérendrye, he was entitled to be paid first, and he asked that the trader's furs be seized at Mackinac for this purpose with an accompanying order to restrain the Sieur Dailleboust from making his collection. Now here was a fine point of constitutional law. The intendant, Hocquart, was supervisor of justice, and it would appear that the jurisdiction was his; but the governor had always exercised general jurisdiction over the posts, and hence had dispensed justice through the post commanders in questions regulating the *voyageurs* in the trade. An appeal was made to both officials, but when the governor, Beauharnois, failed to make a decision, the intendant, after studying the results of an arbitration committee appointed by the parties, issued an ordinance in favor of De Lorme, ordering collection to be made for him.[8]

[4]Varin to Minister, Quebec, May 27, 1740, *Ibid.*, C¹¹A, 74:192-196ᵛ.
[5]Hocquart to Minister, Quebec, Oct. 14, 1742, *Ibid.*, C¹¹A, 78:27-34ᵛ.
[6]Minister to Hocquart, Mar. 7, 1746, *Canadian Archives Reports*, 1899, Supplement, 155. The constant bickering and friction between the governor and the intendant was in keeping with the general condition existing among the officers of the entire bureaucracy, and has been aptly described by Madame Bégon in one of her charming letters to her son as "a terrible jealousy," which she says was as bad in France as in Canada. Madame Bégon to her son, Quebec, Feb. 3, 1750, in *Rapport de l'Archiviste, 1934-1935*, 83. (Cited henceforth as *Quebec Archives Reports*.)
[7]For an example of an appeal of the holder of an expense bill against the intendant's "moderation," though approved by the governor, see "Canada, Démandes Particulières, Feb. 1740," *Arch. Nat., Col.*, C¹¹A, 74:228. In Louisiana, Bienville and Salmon got into such a quarrel over store issues that Salmon asked to be recalled in 1742. Salmon to Minister, Feb. 13, 1742, *Ibid.*, C¹³A, 27:91-92ᵛ.
[8]See Hocquart's *Ordonnance*, in Burpee, *Journals and Letters of La Vérendrye and His Sons*, App., 515-520. Also in *Arch. Nat., Col.*, C¹¹E, 16:240-241ᵛ. Charles, Marquis de Beau-

Beauharnois, incensed over this supposed usurpation of his authority, in a similar case, ordered the commandant at Michilimakinac not to obey Hocquart's order,[9] thus coming to issue with the intendant. The case was then appealed to the minister. Hocquart claimed he was obliged to issue the *ordonnance* in order not to be accused of a denial of justice, and fully established his power to act, by asserting that since the case was one between Montreal merchants it did not concern the governor's jurisdiction in the west. He argued further that he also had the jurisdiction, since the principle that traders should bring their furs down to Montreal was involved. The post commanders might be granted the right to settle cases between *voyageurs*, but this was a different case. Furthermore, he contended the intendant had actual legal jurisdiction over the posts, through his power to appoint sub-delegates.[10] Beauharnois, on the other hand, argued (from the custom) that the *voyageur* must be free in his post, and that the post commandant acting under the governor would do justice in cases arising between him and the merchants.[11] The case was finally dropped when Beauharnois had justice done.

Canada was divided into three chief administrative jurisdictions— Quebec, Montreal, and Three Rivers. The governor general and the intendant had their seats of authority at the city of Quebec, capital of the province of that name. Here, too, was the seat of the local jurisdiction of the city and the surrounding settlements. The jurisdiction of Quebec also extended in certain respects to the control of Isle Royale[12] and the eastern regions about the lower St. Lawrence. Next came the city of Montreal and its district, having a similar jurisdiction. At Montreal sat the governor of the district who stood second to the governor-general at Quebec, though his authority ceased when the governor-general entered the Montreal jurisdiction. A sub-delegate of the intendant, who was the chief commissary of the king's magazines there, was also stationed at Montreal. The Montreal jurisdiction included the city and the nearby settlements, and indirectly the several western posts, for these posts relied directly upon the Montreal commissary for their supplies, just as Isle Royale and the eastern posts were dependent upon Quebec.[13] The commandants and troops, however, were directly under the governor general's control. Each of these districts had a military commander, called the lieutenant of the king in the case of Quebec, and major in the case of

---

harnois, governor-general of New France from 1726 to 1747, was born about 1670, and was trained for the navy. Returning to France in 1747, he became lieutenant-general of naval forces. He died in 1749. Gilles Hocquart was intendant of Canada from 1728 to 1748. He was noted for his energy and integrity.
[9]Beauharnois to Minister, Quebec, Oct. 7, 1740, *Ibid.*, C¹¹A, 74:36-39.
[10]Hocquart to Maurepas, Quebec, Sept. 27, 1741, Burpee, *op. cit.*, 524-530.
[11]Beauharnois to Minister, Quebec, Oct. 7, 1740, *Arch. Nat., Col.*, C¹¹A, 74:36-39.
[12]Isle Royale had a council of its own, and was developing a somewhat separate status. For location of posts and settlements, see map, p. 8, above.
[13]Isle Royale also had an intendant of her own, who was subject to the intendant at Quebec. The policy of the government was that Canada should eventually supply the fortress there with most of its needs.

Montreal and Three Rivers. There were also judicial and police officials. Three Rivers had a similar organization and controlled the forts of Chambly and St. Frederic.

Louisiana was divided into nine military districts, but the three chief establishments—New Orleans, Mobile, and the Illinois—became the real centers of administration. Thus Mobile came to control the posts of the Alabama and Tombechbee, while the Illinois controlled the Arkansas post and the post at Natchitoches. New Orleans had the immediate jurisdiction of the posts at La Pointe Coupée and the Natchez. In the Illinois and at the Mobile post we find the evolution of a deputy intendant and sub-governor in progress. Each of these posts had a deputy of the *ordonnateur*,[14] while the commandants of advanced rank acted as deputy governors.

The army was the chief arm of the governor for defense and maintenance of the administration. At times, too, he had ships at his command, especially in time of war when the king's ships were in colonial ports. Canada, however, had a few small ships of her own.[15]

The number of troops was not large. Of the regulars, or "troops of the Marine," there seem to have been fewer than 1,000 in 1749.[16] Louisiana in 1744 had thirty companies on the rolls.[17] Canada kept her troops stationed chiefly at Montreal and Quebec, Montreal alone having nineteen companies in the year 1741.[18] The western posts rarely had more than small detachments of troops, excepting the Illinois which usually kept two companies.[19]

Officers were appointed by the king upon recommendation of the governors, who usually acted upon the testimonies of their officers, but solicitations of influential family members and others interested in a man's promotion, both in France and in Canada, figured largely. Promotions were not always regular and according to seniority and merit.[20]

Each colony also had its militia organization, officered by men commissioned by the governor, and embracing all able-bodied men, but the

---

[14]In Louisiana the intendant was called the *ordonnateur*, or *commissaire-ordonnateur*.
[15]Shipbuilding was encouraged by the government at Quebec. Several small ships had been built there already, and Maurepas had three armed vessels laid down there during the decade under consideration. There seems to have been little or no private shipbuilding.
[16]This did not count the garrison at Isle Royale, which contained at least as many more men. In 1749, twenty-eight companies of 812 men made up all other Canadian regular troops. See King's Instructions to La Jonquière, 1749, *Arch. Nat., Col.*, B, 89:50ᵛ-51. The same year La Galissonière had recommended that the number be increased to 1,200 French and 200 Swiss. This was approved and officers from Canada were sent to France to take charge of recruiting. Minister to La Jonquière and Bigot, May, 1749, *Can. Arch. Rep.*, 1905, 1, 117.
[17]*Bordereau*, 1744, *Arch. Nat., Col.*, C¹³A, 28:368ᵛ-369. Louisiana got twenty-four new companies in 1750, but these were largely for replacements. Vaudreuil to Minister, Sept. 24, 1750, *Ibid.*, C¹³A, 34:276-277. The *Memoir on Louisiana in 1746* gives the number of troops in the colony as 900. *Ibid.*, C¹³A, 30:256-257. Each company regularly numbered fifty men.
[18]*Bordereau*, 1741, *Ibid.*, C¹¹A, 114:383.
[19]*Petite Mémoire de Canada*, 1744, *Ibid.*, C¹¹A, 78-319.
[20]We even find an instance of a wife asking for the promotion of her husband. See Mme. Longueuil to Minister, Nov. 2, 1747, *Arch. Nat., Col.*, C¹¹A, 89:252-253. An important family in Canada such as that of the Sieur De La Ronde had great influence in obtaining favors of these and other kinds. See Denys de La Ronde to Minister, Quebec, Nov. 12, 1740, *Ibid.*, C¹¹A, 74:216-217; La Jonquière to Minister, Quebec, Nov. 4, 1749, in *Wisconsin Historical Collections*, XVIII, 35-36.

militia on the whole was poorly equipped and trained. Beauharnois had adopted the practice of sending out an officer each year to cause the militia to take their drills.[21] One of the chief difficulties was the obtaining of arms for the use of the troops. The king had recommended that arms be procured in Canada out of proceeds from the licenses of the fur trade, but this had not worked well. The governor reported that even had the money been at hand, no such quantity of guns could be supplied by the merchants.[22] The king then undertook to supply guns, and by 1749 it was reported that 10,000 muskets had been provided. The number of the Canadian militia is given as 12,000.[23] Louisiana with a total population of only 8,000 must have had only a small number.

On the whole the morale and discipline of the troops were not good. The loss of Louisbourg to the English in 1745 was ascribed by many to the insubordination of the troops, while the so-called "Bad Bread Mutiny" in New Orleans at the same time indicated the state of affairs in Louisiana.[24] The prevailing system of quartering troops with the civilian population led to many irregularities, while soldiers stationed in small numbers at the distant posts, or assigned as laborers on projects such as the iron foundry at St. Maurice, were often tempted to desert and become *coureurs de bois* or other fugitives.[25] The number of desertions was constantly increasing, especially in the Illinois, where in the single year of 1742 it was reported that sixteen men had deserted from the two companies quartered there.[26] Ordinarily Canada required sixty men per year as replacements for vacancies in the ranks due largely to desertion.[27] At some of the establishments, however, better order prevailed, this being particularly true of Fort St. Frederic, which Peter Kalm visited in 1749, and where he tells us he found both order and contentment among the troops.[28]

The government did much to eradicate the bad conditions existing among the armed forces. As a general policy, older men were placed in

---

[21]Memoir of the King to Beauharnois and Hocquart, Fontainebleau, Apr. 30, 1742, *Arch. Nat., Col.*, B, 74:503-511.
[22]Beauharnois and Hocquart to Minister, Quebec, undated, *Ibid.*, C¹¹A, 81:34ᵛ-36.
[23]King's Instructions to La Jonquière, Versailles, 1749, *Ibid.*, B, 89:50ᵛ-51.
[24]See records of the trial of the mutineers, in Records of the Superior Council, *Louisiana Historical Quarterly*, XIV, 2, 263-267.
[25]Beauharnois to Minister, Quebec, Oct. 6, 1740, *Arch. Nat., Col.*, C¹¹A, 74:30-33.
[26]Bienville to Minister, New Orleans, Feb. 14, 1743, *Ibid.*, C¹³A, 28:34-34ᵛ.
[27]Memoir of the King to Beauharnois and Hocquart, Fontainebleau, Apr. 30, 1742, *Ibid.*, B, 74:503-511.
[28]Kalm says of the soldiers there: "They get every day a pound and a half of wheat bread, which is almost more than they can eat. They likewise get pease, bacon, and salt meat in plenty .... Each soldier got a new coat every two years; but annually, a waistcoat, cap, hat, breeches, cravat, two pair of stockings, two pair of shoes, and as much wood as he had occasion for in the winter. They likewise got five *sols* a piece every day; which is augmented to thirty sols when they have any particular labour for the King."—*Travels into North America*, III, 16-20. From the Louisiana *Bordereau* for 1745, we learn the following concerning the pay of troops: captains, 90 livres per month; lieutenants, 60 livres; ensigns, 40 livres; ensigns in second, 30 livres; sergeants, 16 livres; corporals, 6 livres, 15 sols; cadets, 12 livres, 15 sols; and the common soldiers, 4 livres, 10 sols. *Arch. Nat., Col.*, C¹³A, 29:240-241. Another authority gives the pay of the common soldier (1747) as 5 deniers *per diem*, and that of ensigns as 10 écus (30 livres) per month. Captains were said to receive 100 livres per month. Lantinac's testimony, *South Carolina Council Minutes*, Apr. 14?, 1747, 83-84, Public Record Office, Colonial Office, 5, v. 455.

the garrisons, and after the expiration of their term of service, they were given land, tools, and livestock so that they might become permanent settlers in the vicinity of the fort.[29] Vaudreuil advocated shifting of post garrisons yearly, a policy which was approved in 1744, but the expense involved kept this from being done.[30] The same system was approved for Canada in 1750.[31] An attempt was also made to remove irregularities in payment of soldiers and officers, especially at the more distant posts. Louisiana in 1746 was permitted to establish the practice of allowing officers to receive half of their pay in letters of exchange.[32] In Canada, where the gratifications of officers at the posts usually depended upon the income of the posts from the fur trade, La Galisonière pleaded for a system of regular pay to enable the officers to keep in better state. In 1740 bad conditions in the distribution of pay to both officers and men were disclosed in a controversy which arose between M. de Noyan, commandant at Detroit, and the office of the Montreal commissary.[33]

The post commandant was a detached officer. For the more important posts, he usually held the rank of captain. In Louisiana the commandants of the Illinois and at Mobile were termed majors. This title was also set up at Detroit under the new system of sedentary command established there in 1749.

In one respect the powers of the post commandant differed in Louisiana from those of the Canadian officer—the Louisiana officer, with the exception of the Illinois commandant, had complete charge of the fur trade at his post. He issued the trading permits, regulated the transportation of goods, and so on. Indeed, he was often a trader himself. In Canada, the control of the trade was in the hands of the intendant at Quebec, officers usually being forbidden to trade.[34] The commandant also was in immediate control of the king's domain, of the king's magazines, and of the regulation of justice in such posts as were not provided with a deputy of the intendant. Officers at such commands as Detroit, Mobile, and the Illinois received gratifications up to 3,000 livres. Sometimes there were special gratifications up to 1,000 livres in addition to the regular pay.[35] In the western posts, this expense was usually paid out

---

[29]Kalm, *op. cit.*, 16-20.
[30]Minister to Vaudreuil, Versailles, Jan. 1, 1744, *Arch. Nat., Col.*, B, 78:3. Pierre François Rigaud de Cavagnol, Marquis de Vaudreuil (1698-1793), was governor of Three Rivers in 1733; becoming governor of Louisiana in 1743, he served there until 1753, when he became governor-general of all New France, holding this position until the end of the French Régime.
[31]King to La Jonquière, Apr. 11, 1744, *Can. Arch. Rep.*, 1905, 1, 131.
[32]Minister to Vaudreuil, Versailles, Apr. 25, 1746, *Arch. Nat., Col.*, B, 83:10ᵛ.
[33]La Galissonière to Minister, Oct. 11, 1747, *Ibid.*, C¹¹A, 87:238. The regimental pay of officers did not depend upon fur trade revenues. The correspondence over this matter is printed in the Cadillac Papers, *Michigan Pioneer and Historical Collection*, 34, 165 ff. Delays in pay were common to soldiers on detached service at distant posts. One soldier is mentioned who had received no pay for three years.
[34]It should be pointed out that some Canadian officers were traders through this period. La Vérendrye is an example. The power of the Canadian governor to issue trading permits for the Illinois posts should be noted as an exception to the general practice of post commanders controlling the trade in Louisiana.
[35]Canada, *Bordereau, 1741*, *Arch. Nat., Col.*, C¹¹A, 114:383ᵛ-384.

of revenues drawn from the fur trade. Some posts had also a second in command.[36] Other officials at the posts were the *aumônier*, or chaplain, the surgeon, the interpreter, the missionary, and the storekeeper, or *garde magazin* as he was called. Sometimes the king kept a smith also, but this right was often given to the missionary as his *ferme*. The tendency at the larger posts was to transform the *garde magazin* into a sub-delegate of the intendant, the post commander correspondingly becoming a deputy governor. In the Illinois and at Detroit this transformation had already taken place by 1750. At the former post, the office of *écrivain principal* had already been established and entrusted with legal jurisdiction in that country as well as some oversight of financial matters. At Detroit a sub-delegate of the intendant resided with similar powers.

To assist the governor and the intendant in the government of the colony, there had been established a council, composed of councilors drawn from the citizenry and appointed by the king. This council consisted of the governor, the intendant, who served as chief justice, the bishop (in Canada), the lieutenant of the king, the attorney general, the clerk (notary), and a number of councilors. There also sat with it or participated in its sessions at times, the sheriff and his deputies, different attorneys, such as attorneys for vacant estates, the agent for the Company of the Indies, the keeper of the king's warehouses, and sometimes sub-delegates of the intendant as well as post officers.[37] These men (the councilors) were on the civil list at small gratifications, all below 1,000 livres in the case of Canada.[38] In 1742, new officials, called assessors, were added to the councils, four to each council. They served as special judges in certain cases, and it was provided that they might vote in other decisions in case of a tie of votes.[39]

The registration of edicts and ordinances of the king as well as those of the governor and intendant was the first duty of the council.[40] It also served in an ordinary advisory capacity to the heads of the administration. But its chief business was as a court of law, both in original and appellate jurisdiction, for the entire colony. It also registered contracts, wills, and

---

[36]Minister to Beauharnois, Versailles, Apr. 30, 1743, *Ibid.*, B, 76:403ᵛ.
[37]The following persons participated in the work of the Superior Council of Louisiana during April and May, 1748: Pierre Rigaud de Vaudreuil, Governor; Vincent D'Auberville, Intendant; Jean Baptiste Raguet, Acting Procureur General; Nicolas Chauvin de Lafrenière, Councillor; Louis Césaire Le Bretton, Councillor Assessor; Charles de la Lande d'Aprémont, Councillor Assessor; Jean François Huchet de Kernion, Councillor Assessor; Gilles Augustin Payen de Noyan, Lieutenant of the King; Nicolas Henry, Clerk and Notary; Austin Chantalon, Sheriff; Marin Le Normand, Deputy Sheriff; The Chevalier de Mambrede, Major of New Orleans; Jean Baptiste Prévost, Agent of the Company of the Indies; Jean Joseph Delfau de Pontalba, Commandant at La Pointe Coupée; Claude Trenaunay de Chanfret, Judge and Sub-delegate at La Pointe Coupée; Bernard Louis Petin, Notary at La Pointe Coupée; Pierre Olivier Devezin, Surveyor of the King's Highways; Nicolas Godefroy Barbin, Attorney of Vacant Estates; Jean Baptiste Gavic, Attorney. Rec. of the Sup. Coun., *La. Hist. Quart.*, XIX, 3, 751. For a complete list of members of the Canadian Council, see P. G. Roy, "Les Conseillers du Conseil Souverain de la Nouvelle France," *Trans. Roy. Soc. of Canada*, third ser., IX, 173-187.
[38]*Bordereau*, 1741, Arch. Nat., Col., C¹¹A, 115:11ᵛ-12. Of course, these councilors, being legal professionists, were able to increase their incomes.
[39]*Edits, Ordonnances*, I, 561-563.
[40]*Ibid.*, 588.

other legal documents through its notary.[41] Appeals from the decisions of the superior council could be made only to the king.[42]

As a superior court of justice the council spent a great deal of its time in hearing cases both civil and criminal—cases on appeal as well as those of original jurisdiction. Under the direction of the intendant judges were sent into the distant settlements where they held court in the stead of the council. Appeals from the decisions of these judges returned to the council for final review. In no case was there trial by jury, but the judges alone decided the cases in accordance with the *coutume de Paris*.

Sometimes the intendant had to form special courts to hear cases of an unusual nature. Thus, in 1741, when a case in admiralty arose at New Orleans, M. Salmon, after consulting the attorney general on the subject, constituted himself into an admiralty court and heard the case.[43] The *seigneurs* also had once possessed the right to hold courts on their domains, though this right had been nominally abolished in 1693. For the convenience of the reader there is listed below an outline of the legal jurisdictions of Montreal with the officers and justices according to rank. The pay of judges, sheriffs, sergeants, etc., was based on the type of the case handled, the time spent, distances travelled, and so on.[44]

We have referred above to the office of *écrivain principal* in the Illinois. Due to the great distance of this region from New Orleans, this office had been created, and an officer sent there *"en qualité de subdélégué de l'ordonnateur."* He had jurisdiction over any case arising in that country, but appeals from his decisions could be made to the council at

---

[41]For samples of various registrations made by the council, see *La. Hist. Quart.*, X, 2, etc.
[42]The decrees of the council covered subjects all the way from ordinances against snowballing of people on the streets of Montreal to an ordinance regulating the length of cord-wood. See Council Records in the various volumes of the *La. Hist. Quart.* and the *Edits, Ordonnances*. The records of the Quebec council are printed separately.
[43]See De Meyere v. Du Conge, in *La. Hist. Quart.*, VII, 1, 1-19. Edmé Gatien Salmon was intendant of Louisiana, 1731-1743.
[44]Outline of officials of justice and jurisdictions at Montreal:
I. Seigneurial justice (1648-1693; abolished Nov. 15, 1693. Some seigneurs about Montreal still exercised some judicial authority, however).
    a. Judges, judges of bailiwicks, lieutenants (civil and criminal).
    b. Secondary judges (usually used in absence of the regular judges, they being often garrison officers).
    c. Fiscal procureurs.
    d. Substitutes for fiscal procureurs.
    e. Notaries (regular).
    f. Special notaries or notarial agents.
    g. Huissiers and sergeants.
    h. Jailors and prison keepers.
    i. Assessors (advisors to judges).
    j. Interpreters.
    k. Tabellions and other notaries.
II. First royal justice, or Sénéchaussée (created Sept. 28, 1663). Composed of a civil and criminal judge, an attorney of the king, a greffier and royal notary, and a royal sergeant.
III. Second royal justice, or Prévôté (the council) (1693-1760). Composed of the lieutenant general of Montreal, the king's attorney, a greffier, four royal notaries, four huissiers, and four advocates. The complete list of officers attached to the council at Montreal was:
    a. Lieutenants, civil and criminal.
    b. Lieutenants in second.
    c. Special lieutenants to assist the above.
    d. The king's attorneys.
    e. Assistant attorneys.
    f. Greffiers for military courts.
    g. Greffiers and assistants.
    h. Huissiers of the king.
    i. Jailors and prison keepers.
    j. Assessors.
    k. Interpreters.
    l. Royal notaries.
    m. Special advocates.
    n. Commissaries.
    o. Deputy intendants and their notaries.
    p. Maréchaussée (Prévost marshal's lieutenant).
Massicote, E.-Z., "Tribunaux et Officiers de Justice....," *Trans. Roy. Soc. of Canada*, third ser., X, 273-303. For list of fees collected by these officers in the several different cases, see *Edits, Ordonnances*, I, 609-611.

New Orleans. This was the only definitely organized inferior jurisdiction in Louisiana, though a separate jurisdiction for the city of New Orleans was under consideration.[45] The *écrivain principal* was also a *functionaire* over the king's stores at the Illinois, and the *garde magazin* logically succeeded him.[46] In trifling matters below the notice of the judges, the local priest or the commandant of the post usually brought about a settlement between the parties to the litigation.

In keeping with the times, the law was harsh. Imprisonment for debt was common,[47] and torture was used to extort confessions, especially in case of negroes.[48] Under the Black Code, the punishment of negroes was severe. A slave who struck a soldier in 1742 was condemned to be whipped every week day and on Sundays at a certain place in the city of New Orleans by the public executioner, to have his right ear cut off, and to carry a six-pound ball on his foot for the remainder of his days.[49] Slaves who were manumitted could be easily reduced to slavery if they failed to pay their debts.[50] Fines were eagerly laid upon offenders and collected with rigour. Justice was also expensive. Judge Breese cites a case tried in the Illinois in 1749 involving a suit for collection of a note of the value of 60 livres in which the costs of the suit amounted to the sum of 28 livres, 10 sols.[51]

There remains to be discussed the office of notary under the French colonial system. This official heard cases such as are now handled by our courts or judges, while at the same time he performed the duties of our notaries public, common magistrates, and justices of the peace. Notaries were of two kinds: *royal* and *seigneurial*. The tendency since 1669 had been to restrict the latter, for after that year all nominations of *seigneurial* notaries were made subject to the approval of the intendant.[52] In the absence of the notary, his duties might be performed by the judge, the missionary, the military commandant, or even by the *garde magazin*.[53] In rank and dignity the notary stood next to the royal officers.[54]

---

[45]Memoir of the King to M. Michel, Versailles, Dec. 9, 1748, *Arch. Nat., Col.*, D, 0/.20. The jurisdiction of the sub-delegate was broad enough to cover even murder cases. See case of one Marie Jeanne, a slave, tried for infanticide in 1748. The case was first brought before Sieur Joseph Buchet, the royal storekeeper in the Illinois. Rec. of the Sup. Coun., *La. Hist. Quart.*, XIX, 4, 1112-1115.
[46]Thus when the Sieur La Loere Flaucourt died in that capacity in 1747, the Sieur Buchet, *garde magazin* at Kaskaskia succeeded him. Minister to Sr. Buchet, Versailles, Dec. 11, 1747, *Arch. Nat., Col.*, B, 85:32.
[47]See case in *La. Hist. Quart.*, VII, 4, 555-556.
[48]*Ibid.*, XIII, 1, 122-123.
[49]*Ibid.*, XI, 2, 292.
[50]*Ibid.*, XVIII, 1, 168. For a copy of the Black Code, see *Receuils de Règlemens, Edits Declarations et Arrêts, Concernant la Commerce, l'Administration de justice, et la Police de colonies Françaises de l'Amérique, et les Engagés. Avec le Code Noir*, Paris, 1765. Also see Riddell, Hon. William Renwick, "Le Code Noir," *Trans. Royal Soc. of Canada*, third ser., XIX, Sec. II, 33-38.
[51]Breese, S. J., *The Early History of Illinois*, 49.
[52]*Quebec Archives, Reports*, 1921-1922, P. G. Roy, 1 ff. The best treatise on the French notariat is that by P. G. Roy, entitled *Histoire du Notariat au Canada*, 4 vols., Levis, 1890.
[53]*La. Hist. Quart.*, XIII, 4, 672; XIII, 2, 515.
[54]See Hocquart's ordinance in a case involving the question of precedence of notaries over other officials at church. *Edits, Ordonnances*, II, 553.

All notaries were required to keep registers of their acts which became record books for the use of the notary himself as well as for the judges and the intendant at their need. At certain times the king's attorneys inspected these registers to see that they were in due form, and a notary who consisently failed to comply with regulations was expelled from office.[55]

The form of notarial acts was also regulated by a royal edict. All acts were to be signed under oath by the parties concerned as well as by proper witnesses. Details concerning the parties, their domicile, their names, and the date of the act, were given most minutely, and in cases in which property was involved, the fullest details of all liens and other instruments were required.[56] By an ordinance of 1743 the notary was also required to keep a minute book in addition to his register.[57]

Notaries, like judges, were paid on the basis of fees collected. When a minute of an act was required, the charge was double what it was without the minute. The pay of subaltern notaries was half that of the royal notaries.[58]

Notarial acts were many and various, involving such things as the following: collection of debts, drawing up of wills and testaments, business contracts, marriages, deeds and transactions, sales, inventories and chancery acts, papers of apprenticeship, registration of gifts and donations, duty of coroner, acts of supervision of minors, etc.[59] Notarial acts were often registered directly with the superior council, though this was not necessary. The council, of course, had a notary who registered its own acts.

This officer, then, filled an important place in the French judicial system, being vastly more important than our *notary public* of today. The office was evidently sold at a high price, a case having been cited in which a buyer sues to get possession of his registers after having, as it seems, paid 10,000 livres for the office.[60]

Relations between church and state in the French American colonies present an interesting study. Canada was well supplied with religious organizations. There were two seminaries, one at Quebec conducted by the priests of the *Missions Etrangères,* and one at Montreal under the Sulpicians. The Jesuits also had their college at Quebec—the only college in New France. The priests of the Quebec seminary supplied most of the parishes of Canada, those at Montreal ministering to that community only. There were minor schools to prepare persons for the orders at

---

[55]See Edict of Aug. 2, 1717, *Edits, Ordonnances,* I, 372-375.
[56]*Edits, Ordonnances,* I, 539-541.
[57]*Ibid.,* II, 386.
[58]Here are samples of notarial fees: for an obligation below 20 livres, 5 sols; for an agreement of apprenticeship with minute, 20 sols; for copy of act on paper, 6 sols; for same on parchment, 20 sols. *Ibid.,* I, 611-612.
[59]The Canadian notarial registers have been calendared in *Quebec Archives.* The records of the councils also give much light on notarial acts.
[60]See *La. Hist. Quart.,* X, 1, 81-85.

Quebec and St. Joachim. In each of the cities—Quebec, Montreal, and Three Rivers—there was a convent of Recollets and a hospital served by the Ursulines; there was also a *hôpital général* at Quebec. The Recollets sometimes went among the Indians, though they generally served as chaplains in the army and on the king's ships. There were no other orders of monks established in Canada besides these.[61] The Jesuits also had a church at Montreal, as well as the Franciscans, and each city had a nunnery. At Montreal also was the order of *Soeurs de Congrégation,* who were not nuns, but who worked among the people, teaching reading and writing, and doing charitable deeds.[62] The parishes of Louisiana were served by the Capuchins of Champagne. New Orleans, too, had a hospital served by the Ursulines.[63]

In both Louisiana and Canada the Jesuits served the missions among the Indians with a few exceptions. At the Lake of the Two Mountains situated at the mouth of the Ottawa River, the Sulpicians had a mission, while the *Missions Etrangères* had been given a field in the Illinois country, to which they still held title, but which they did not work actively.

The government heavily subsidized all these religious foundations. In Louisiana in 1744, the king allowed 16,104 livres for this item, not counting the support of the Ursulines in the hospital at New Orleans.[64] Canada, having a much larger religious foundation, got 57,200 livres from the king for its suport in 1741.[65] Missionaries among the Indians were allowed 600 livres yearly by the king.

Education in the colonies was in the hands of the church, though a few men interested in the higher sciences worked independently. La Galissonière was greatly interested in natural history and did much for its advancement. He worked on lists of the plants, animals, and minerals of the colony, and had all post officers instructed to help him in collecting

---

[61] See King's Instructions to La Jonquière, Apr. 30, 1749, Versailles, *Arch. Nat., Col.,* B, 89:49v-50; Kalm, *op. cit.,* III, 144-149. Kalm gives the best description of the Canadian religious institutions.

[62] Kalm, *op. cit.,* III, 72-74; 304-305.

[63] Memoir of the King for Instructions for M. Michel, Versailles, Dec. 9, 1748, *Arch. Nat., Col.,* B, 87:27. The Capuchins in Louisiana in 1750 were distributed as follows: Five at New Orleans (one being senile), one at Mobile, one "au Appaloches," two at the German Coast, one at La Pointe Coupée, one at Natchez, and one at Natchitoches. La Balize was vacant, the church there being *hors d'état.* L'Abbé de L'Isle Dieu to Pontbriand, Apr. 4, 1750, *Quebec Arch. Rep.,* 1935-36, 298-299. There were also a number of Jesuits serving in Louisiana, there being in 1749 five at the different Illinois settlements (two of these were old), two among the Choctaw, and two at New Orleans, one in the position of superior and grand vicar and the other as almoner at the military hospital. L'Abbé de L'Isle Dieu to President of the Council of Marine, Paris, Mar. 28, 1752, *Ibid.,* 322.

[64] *Bordereau,* 1744, *Arch. Nat., Col.,* C13A, 28:368v-369.

[65] See King's Statement, 1741, *Ibid.,* C11A, 115:10-13. These subsidies were not, however, regularly paid. The Abbé de L'Isle Dieu, writing to Bishop Pontbriand, speaks of the debts of the *Filles de la Congrégation* at Louisbourg, saying: "And why are they in debt? Because the king has paid them nothing of their pension of 1500 livres since 1743 and there was due them in the month of January last six years (pension) making a total of 9,000 livres." Abbé de L'Isle Dieu to Pontbriand, Apr. 4, 1750, *Quebec Arch. Rep.,* 1935-36, 300. The Abbé had succeeded in collecting 1640 livres of this when he wrote. Pierre de la Rue, Abbé de L'Isle Dieu (1688-1799), was vicar-general of Quebec, 1734-1777. See also L'Abbé de L'Isle Dieu to President of Council of Marine, Apr. 21, 1747, *Quebec Arch. Rep.,* 1935-36, 281; same to same, Sept. 12, 1747, *Ibid.,* 282-284. At this time the religious establishments on Isle Royale had received nothing of the subsidies promised them, while the Ursulines in New Orleans were hardly better off. In 1746, Father Charlevoix reported that the Ursulines at New Orleans had failed to receive the full subsidies allotted them for three years, the total arrears amounting to 21,679 livres, 10 sols. L'Abbé de L'Isle Dieu to Pontbriand, Feb. 2, 1746, *Quebec Arch. Rep.,* 1935-36, 279-280.

specimens for the royal gardens at Versailles. It was he who invited Kalm to Canada, at government expense, and entertained him during his studies there.[66] But outside this small circle, the clergymen and official class, learning was not greatly pursued in the colony. The fact that a colony of 80,000 people owned not a single printing press, may be an index to this, at a time when the newspaper flourished in nearly all the New England colonies. Even the home government, in answer to La Galissonière's request for a press, had not deemed it necessary.[67]

In return for his subsidies to the church, the king expected it to bend to his control. Regulation of the religious houses was very strict, and their right to own and hold land was carefully controlled.[68] In case of controversy over property held by the church, the king usually stepped in and sometimes took over the property in dispute. Thus in 1744, during a controversy over the repair of the bishop's palace in Quebec, the king advanced the amount needed and annexed the palace and grounds to his domain, allowing the bishop to use them free of charge.[69] The superior council kept peace in case of disputes also. A famous case is the controversy over raising of pew rents in New Orleans in 1747.[70] On the other hand, the government supported the church against its enemies, and helped it when it was in trouble. When a new church edifice was being built, and parishioners lagged in their duty, the ecclesiastical authorities could easily secure an edict from the council, ordering them to carry out their obligations,[71] and heretics or profaners of religion were punished by the state.[72] Generally speaking, the church maintained an undisputed hold on the people. According to Kalm the religious atmosphere in Canada was much more intense than in the English colonies.[73]

In respect to the question of the liquor trade with the Indians, however, the state and church were in continuous conflict. The new bishop, Pontbriand, who came over in 1742, took the same stand on this question that his predecessors had taken. Regarding the liquor traffic among the savages the government had long maintained its necessity, on the ground that it could not be prohibited without corresponding loss of furs to the English. It was further subtly proposed by the govern-

---

[66]Kalm, *op. cit.*, III, 5-7.
[67]Minister to La Jonquière, May 4, 1749, *Can. Arch. Rep.*, 1899, Sup., 159. See also Kalm, *op. cit.*, III, 182. There had been a press in Canada earlier.
[68]*Edits, Ordonnances*, I, 576-581. In some cases friction between the government and a religious institution was accentuated by the enmity of royal officials. Thus in 1746, Le Normand, the stormy intendant of Louisiana, practically destroyed the power of the Ursulines by his restrictive measures against them. There may be some relationship between Le Normand's enmity for this order and their failure to receive the royal subsidies in this period. L'Abbé de L'Isle Dieu to Pontbriand, Feb. 2, 1746, *Quebec Arch., Rep.*, 1935-36, 279-280. This same official also waged war on the Jesuits. The high officials of the church, however, were cognizant of the position of the church, and grateful for the government's good-will. Both sides realized the importance of the missionary as a power with the Indians politically. *Ibid.*
[69]*Edits, Ordonnances*, I, 568-571.
[70]See *La. Hist. Quart.*, II, 365-367.
[71]*Edits, Ordonnances*, III, Mar. 27, 1745, 347-348.
[72]In the case of a fortune teller who used the crucifix and the New Testament, a sentence of three years in the galleys and a scourging was imposed. *Can. Arch. Rep.*, 1899, 151.
[73]Kalm, *op. cit.*, III, 80 ff. Kalm gives in these pages a vivid description of the wayside crosses in Canada.

ment that a loss in trade would also be detrimental to the interests of religion; for when the Indians would go to trade with the English, they would also imbibe English heresies. The happy medium, therefore, according to this argument, was to tolerate the liquor trade and seek only to keep down abuses.[74] Pontbriand, however, could not conscientiously agree to this policy. In a scholarly argument he sought to prove that liquor was not as important in holding the trade of the Indians as the introduction of better and cheaper merchandise. From the spiritual side, he opined that the trade in liquor was "absolutely contrary to Christianity."

He complained bitterly that the officers of the posts made little attempt to enforce the regulations on the liquor trade and to limit abuses. Then he went further and took the stand that dealers selling *eau de vie* to the savages should not be absolved of their sins in the confessional, unless they should promise not to repeat the offense. He said concerning this subject: "I would wish with all my heart that religion could agree in this case with the interests of the colony, and that one could trade in *eau de vie* without sin. I would likewise be very much charmed if the most skilled doctors could take away from me the scruples which I can but have on this subject . . . . " At the least he asked for very strict enforcement of prohibition in the jurisdictions of Montreal, Three Rivers, and Quebec, and among the domiciliated Indians.[75] Though the bishop would not yield, he was forced to accept conditions as they were, and the liquor trade went on. In a letter from the Illinois in 1748 we are told that a fifth of the Indians of the Tamarois mission were constantly under the influence of *eau de vie* which the merchants and *voyageurs* sold daily.[76] The government did try to regulate the amount of liquor sent out for the trade. Thus we find that in the case of the contract Vaudreuil made with the Sieur Deruisseau for the Missouri trade in 1744, it was stipulated that there was to be no trade whatsoever in liquor.[77] The amount of liquor going up from Montreal in the *voyageur's* canoes was also carefully regulated.

---

[74]Minister to Pontbriand, Apr. 27, 1742, *Can Arch Rep*, 1904, 304-306. Henri du Breuil de Pontbriand (1769-1760) was Bishop of Quebec, 1741-1760. See also Abbé de L'Isle Dieu to Pontbriand, Paris, Apr. 4, 1750, *Queb. Arch. Rep.*, 1935-36, 296. Here the writer states the thesis that it is necessary to continue the trade, giving the government's case.
[75]Bishop of Quebec to Minister, Aug. 22, 1742, *Arch. Nat., Col.*, C^{11}A, 78:107-109. The Abbé de L'Isle Dieu took a somewhat different stand in admitting the necessity of the liquor. Though he held it necessary to permit the liquor trade with the Indians, he pointed out the necessity of driving out the English traders and supplying of suitable goods to the Indians on the part of the French. He also recommended forbidding trading on the part of soldiers, and placing all trade in the hands of a single company which would maintain central storehouses in Quebec and New Orleans from which all goods for the trade would be distributed. L'Abbé de L'Isle Dieu to Pontbriand, Apr. 17, 1752, *Queb. Arch. Rep.*, 1935-36, 329. The question had been on different occasions referred to the Sorbonne, but all their decisions had been such as to avoid committing themselves. Same to same, Apr., 1750, *Ibid.*, 298.
[76]Abbé de L'Isle Dieu to Minister (?), Dec. 5, 1748, *Arch. Nat., Col.*, C^{11}A, 76:297-297^v. See same to Pontbriand, Feb. 2, 1746, in which it is stated through authority of Father Mercier that the tribes domiciliated there were constantly embroiled by the effects of drink, and often on the brink of revolt against the French. *Quebec Arch. Rep.*, 1935-36, 278. The abandonment of the Choctaw mission in 1747 by the Jesuits, if we are to believe their account, was due quite as much to the bad effects of liquor among the Indians as to the fact that the Choctaw were then in revolt against the French. Same to same, Apr. 4, 1750, *Quebec Arch. Rep.*, 1935-36, 298.
[77]See the memoir on this contract, *Arch. Nat., Col.*, C^{13}A, 28:226^v-332.

The king, however, managed to keep on closer terms with the Jesuits than he did with the bishop; consequently, there was friction between the bishop and that order.[78] Of course the Jesuits did not agree with the government on the liquor trade question. On the whole, however, they were willing to serve the king in a political as well as a religious capacity, and they rendered great services in keeping the Indians loyal to the French and poisoned against the English.[79] Even Beauharnois, with his dislike for the Jesuits, was obliged to say: "I have never denied that the influence of the missionaries over the minds of the Indians .... could greatly contribute to the advantages to be expected from them .... "[80] The influence of the Jesuits on the savages was in most cases very great, especially among those who were domiciliated. In 1749 the society had a total of fifty-one members in New France, thirty-four of whom were priests located chiefly among the Indians at the various missions.[81]

The finances of New France were a part of those of the mother country, and were supplied through the treasurer general of the marine, whose office was at Rochefort. The unit of value as fixed in 1726 was the *livre tournois*, worth one *franc*, two *centimes* in terms of the 1914 French currency. At the same time the gold mark had been fixed at 740 livres, 9 sols, 1 denier, and the silver mark at 51 livres, 3 sols, 3 deniers. Government revenues were "farmed" to forty men called farmers general who established a fund of 60,000,000 livres by advancing 1,500,000 livres each. They made a contract with the government for a six-year period by the terms of which they were to turn in a certain amount of cash each year. In 1744 this amount was set at 92,000,000 livres and in 1749, at 101,000,000 livres. All collected above this amount went as profit to the farmers.[82]

In New France the circulating medium was chiefly paper. Foreign coins, French coins, coins issued by trading companies, and some few coins minted especially for the colonies circulated to a small extent.[83] Coin, however, was always rare, due to the unfavorable trade balance against the colonies, and the reluctance of France to send over coin in any case because of fear of losses in war, or by shipwreck. The common circulating medium was thus restricted to the issues of card money, usually greatly depreciated, bills of exchange on the treasury at Rochefort,

---

[78]Kalm, *op. cit.*, III, 143-144. See also the quarrel between the Jesuits and the bishop in 1750, when the Jesuits gave refuge to a priest who was under the bishop's ban. They threatened an appeal to Paris and Rome on the subject and brought the bishop to terms. *Journal des pp. Jesuites*, in Thwaites, *Jes. Rel.*, 69, 237.
[79]Kalm, *op. cit.*, III, 142.
[80]Beauharnois to Minister, October 8, 1744, *Doc. Rel. to the Col. Hist. of N. Y.*, IX, 1108-1109.
[81]"Catalogue of the Persons and Offices of the Society of Jesus, for the Province of France, at the end of the year 1749," Thwaites, *Jes. Rel.*, 69, 74-79.
[82]Lavisse, E., *Histoire de France*, VIII, 2, 95 ff.; 229 ff. Twenty sols made 1 livre, and 12 deniers made 1 sol.
[83]Thompson, C. M., *Monetary System of Nouvelle-France*, 148. Copper coins of small denominations were minted at La Rochelle especially for the colonies and were stamped "Colonies Françaises."

and bills against the local treasury or stores. Bills of trading companies also circulated.[84]

Colonial finances occupy an important place in a study of this period. In Louisiana, by 1744, chiefly as a result of the strain of the Chickasaw War, when great amounts of paper had been issued, card money had fallen into such great disrepute that it was withdrawn from circulation by the king's ordinance.[85] Encouragement of the circulation of Spanish silver *pistoles* then took place, and the false prosperity, due to the war of 1744-1748, led to a boom in trade, especially with the Spanish. Champigny says agriculture was neglected and even comfortable planters left their land to enter commerce.[86] After the peace of 1748, trade rapidly declined and the Spanish money was withdrawn. "It became impossible to maintain the expenses of the colony with such means of exchange and it was necessary to fall back on our miserable old system of paper money."[87]

Expenses of the colony were classified as fixed, or ordinary, and as indefinite, or extraordinary. Together they made up the total of acquittals for the account of the colonies at the treasury of the marine each year.[88] Ordinary expenses were fixed by the king, and included such items as salaries of officials, grants to the religious institutions, sums ordained for the fortifications, and the like. Extraordinary expenses, on the other hand, were determined in the colony by the exigencies of the service. These arose for the most part in connection with war and the Indian administration—they were unforeseen, and hence could not be estimated beforehand. They were ordered by the governor and approved and issued by the intendant in the form of issues from the king's stores, or more often by furnishings of private individuals for the king's account. They rarely involved money, but most often were issues in kind.[89] All expense accounts were visaed by the governor and usually signed by him, but the real issue was in the hands of the intendant, who could "moderate" the total of the bill if he felt it was unjust.[90]

---

[84]Thompson, *op. cit.*, 150. One of the best contemporary accounts of the currency is found in Le Mascrier's edition of Dumont's *Mémoires sur La Louisiane*, II, 53-57. Dumont's manuscript may be found in the Newberry Library in Chicago. The card money was issued in denominations of from 5 sols to 50 livres. Since many people could not read, the denomination was indicated by the manufacture of the card. In the center was printed the royal arms, on one side the number of the card, and on the other the amount and value. These cards were signed by the treasurer, the governor, and the intendant. They were legal tender even on vessels of the king and the company. Counterfeiting was common. The cards could be exchanged in the colonies for bills of exchange on France, but in France they could be exchanged only for Spanish piasters at a great discount, according to Dumont. In 1728, according to the same authority, the piaster was valued at 5 livres French money or 10 écus in cards. Ten years later (after the company had returned Louisiana to the king) the piaster was worth 7 livres, 10 sols, in cards. At the posts nearly all trading was done by barter, money being rarely seen.

[85]Dated Apr. 27, 1744, *Can. Arch. Rep.*, 1899, Sup., 154. French says the circulation reached 7,000,000 livres and circulated at twenty per cent par of specie. This doubtless included paper of all kinds. See Champigny's Memoir on Louisiana, in *La. Hist. Coll.*, V, 135-137. A recent investigator, using the Paris Archives material, gives the paper in circulation in 1744 as 1,050,000 livres. See N. M. Surrey, *The Commerce of Louisiana*, 134.

[86]French, *La. Hist. Coll.*, V, 135-137.

[87]From "A Chapter in Colonial History," in *La. Hist. Quart.*, VI, 4, 567.

[88]Instructions to M. Michel, Versailles, Dec. 9, 1748, *Arch. Nat., Col.*, B, 87:30.

[89]*Ibid.*, 30-30ᵛ.

[90]Minister to Vaudreuil and Le Normand, Versailles, *Ibid.*, B, 83:20-20ᵛ.

Each colony also had extraordinary receipts, which were usually negligible in amount. These included income from sales made from the king's stores to individuals, and the return of goods issued in case of their not being used in the service. The receipts from fees and licenses from the fur trade might also be included under this head, though it was not customary; the same applied to other incomes.[91] The ordinary receipts were the stocks from the king's stores sent from France, and the right to use a certain amount of letters of exchange to augment this sum.

Besides the expenses of the colony within the colony, sometimes incidental expenses were charged to the account of the colony in France. Thus in 1742, M. Salmon asks credit for 20,094 livres, 12 sols, 11 deniers to cover expenses occasioned by troops of the marine from Brest, and some miners sent to his colony.[92] Pensions to colonials also were often paid in France.

Expenses were charged to the funds of the colony in three ways: first, by letters of exchange on the treasurer general at Rochefort; secondly, by the statements of goods furnished by individuals for the service over and above the goods furnished by the king for his stores; and thirdly, by small outlays in France at the colony's account, such as pensions, gratifications, etc. Of the total funds ordained in France for the colony, four deniers per livre were withheld for the general pension fund. Extra letters of exchange beyond the amount decreed formed an anticipation on the account of the colony for the following year.[93]

Each year the king stocked his magazines in the colonies, these supplies being a part of the funds of the colony, and being charged to the colony's account as receipts. The goods were generally bought in France at prices fixed by the intendant at Rochefort. Being delivered by the furnishers to the depots there, they were issued to the colony on proper receipt at fixed prices, quantities, weights, and measures, and then sent to the colony, usually in the king's ships, but sometimes in private vessels. The storekeeper in the colony received the goods and entered the receipts into his registers, and then issued a certificate to the masters of the ships which discharged them and their clerks of the cargoes, and, in the case of private vessels in this service, served also as a freight receipt. The storekeeper and the intendant then made recognition of these receipts upon the general statement for the colony. The farmer general of revenues of that district also had a receipt of the transaction.[94] The regulation of qualities and measures was fixed in an edict of March 1, 1744.[95]

Toward the end of the year, there was drawn up in the colony a

---

[91] Memoir for Instruction for M. Michel, Versailles, Dec. 9, 1748, *Ibid.*, B, 87:31ᵛ.
[92] Salmon to Minister, Feb. 13, 1742, *Ibid.*, C¹³A, 27:91-92ᵛ.
[93] Memoir for Instruction for M. Michel, Versailles, Dec. 9, 1748, *Ibid.*, B, 87:30ᵛ-31ᵛ.
[94] *Ibid.*
[95] *Edits, Ordonnances*, I, 576-585.

bordereau, or general statement of the receipts and expenses of the colony for the year, which was based upon the king's statement issued earlier in the year, plus the receipts for the stores, and extraordinary receipts, against which was set the total expenditures, including letters of exchange drawn for the extraordinary expenses, and total issues in kind, as well as all money spent. The excess over the total allowed in the king's statement was carried forward as an anticipation on the funds of the following year. The agent of the farmer-general in charge of the revenues in the colony issued a statement to the farmer-general showing all letters of exchange and other discharges, which should agree with the sum ordered by the king plus that to be remitted in advance on the expense of the following year.[96] This was the farmer-general's check.

With this explanation of the fiscal system, we shall discuss the expenditures and receipts of the colony of Louisiana during the period under consideration. Unfortunately, the statements of extraordinary expenses seem to be entirely lost, and expense accounts for the whole colony are not at hand for every year. Thus we are handicapped in making any complete analysis of the finances of the colony for the period. We can, however, make sample studies.

Louisiana was returned to the crown by the Company of the Indies in 1731, but it was some years before the settlement was completely made. The king assumed the company's properties there, valued at 445,489 livres, 2 sols, while the company paid the state 1,004,510 livres, 18 sols to be released from its contract.[97] Thus the control of the company came to an end. The Illinois country had been added to Louisiana during the period of the company's control,[98] so that the colony was now increased over its former size and consequently had a larger budget.

It would seem when compared with those of Canada, that the expenses of Louisiana were exceedingly large. This may have been due to the greater inflation of the currency in the early period, and especially to the unusual expenditures in 1739-1740 during the Chickasaw campaign. Bienville and Salmon wrote in June, 1740, that the country was flooded with paper as a result of this undertaking, and they estimated that 200,000 livres in card money would be required to keep up the circulation at the posts.[99]

In 1743 the colony evidently still suffered from the effect of this derangement, for in that year, Vaudreuil (who has been accused of being more extravagant than Bienville) estimated expenses in the colony at

---

[96]Memoir for Instructions for M. Michel, Versailles, *Arch. Nat., Col.*, B, 87:31ᵛ.
[97]See Statement on Retrocession of Louisiana, dated in 1742?, *Ibid.*, C¹³A, 27:185 ff.
[98]*Edits, Ordonnances*, Sept. 27, 1717, I, 388.
[99]Bienville and Salmon to Minister, June 24, 1740, *Arch. Nat., Col.*, C¹³A, 25:9-16ᵛ. The total of expenditures on this campaign is missing, though it was sent with this letter. Jean Baptiste le Moyne, Sieur de Bienville (1680-1768), was founder of Louisiana with Iberville, his brother, and governor, 1702-1704, 1718-1724, 1733-1743.

932,318 livres, 12 sols. He tried to find justification for these large expenditures in the great outlays for fortification, which he says accounted for two-thirds of the amount, but he admits the whole sum had been greatly augmented by the lack of bills of exchange, in lieu of which M. Salmon had been forced to issue paper which the merchants had greatly discredited. He said the only remedy for the situation was to liquidate the outstanding paper as soon as possible. A plan for accomplishing this at least expense to the king was offered in the proposal that 600 negroes be sent over at the king's account, these to be sold at 1,800 livres each, thus retiring all outstanding paper, and giving the king a profit of 360,000 livres besides.[100] The proposal, however, seems not to have been favorably received by the minister.

In 1744, the total receipts for the whole colony were put at 192,610 livres, 1 sol, 9 deniers, to which was to be added sales of goods, and other incomes amounting to 23,512 livres, 14 sols, 3 deniers. But the grand total of expenses amounted to 713,055 livres, 8 sols, 11 deniers, leaving, without counting extraordinary receipts, an anticipation on the next year of 520,445 livres, 7 sols, 2 deniers. This gives some idea of how the inflation of Louisiana currency affected the country's budget. While the 192,610 livres, 1 sol, 9 deniers, represented chiefly receipts from France sent to the king's stores, nearly 400,000 livres extra was expended in purchases in the colony for stocking the same stores. A part of these expenditures were of course due to the war against the Chickasaw, while the outbreak of war with the English also occasioned additional expenses.[101]

In 1745, with conditions improving, the recapitulation was:[102]

	Livres
Appointments of officials, officers, and others	87,290
Gratifications	7,740
Pay and support of companies	77,157
Appointments of *officiers reformés*	2,520
Wages of officers of the marine, sailors, and workers	19,804
Presents to the savages	14,000
Divers expenses	110,738
Fortifications	61,000
Total	380,249

Receipts for this year are not given, and there is reason to suspect that extraordinary expenses might not be included. On the whole, however, it would seem that the financial situation was more stable at this time.

Naturally there were frequent demands for retrenchment. A great deal of criticism was brought against Louisiana because of unusual expenses at the posts. Vaudreuil admitted abuses, but argued that no other

---

[100]Vaudreuil to Minister, New Orleans, Aug. 25, 1743, *Ibid.*, C¹³A, 28:84-84ᵛ.
[101]*Bordereau*, 1744, *Ibid.*, C¹³A, 28:368 ff.
[102]*Bordereau*, 1745, *Ibid.*, C¹³A, 29:237 ff.

method could be used except that of giving receipt for payment at the posts when purchases were made there, and he was not of the opinion that these receipts should be censored later.[103] Another reason for heavier expenses was found in the fact that letters of exchange had customarily been drawn for long terms in Louisiana. In 1746 this was remedied by putting the letters of exchange upon the shortest terms possible.[104]

The amount required for Indian presents constantly increased. The king had allowed at the beginning of this period 14,000 livres for this item, but by 1746 the total amounted to 54,000 livres. This was due in part to war conditions then existing, but it cannot be denied that there were other factors in the increase. It is true that additional presents for the Illinois Indians were necessitated by the uprising among the Indians beginning in 1747. In any case, economy was demanded by the minister.[105]

Great expenses and abuses also existed in the practice of sending up the Illinois convoy each year. This convoy included three or more *batteaux* each manned by a score or more of men, and a number of *pirogues* with crews of eight or nine. By this convoy supplies were sent up to the posts at the Arkansas, at Natchitoches, and the Illinois. The boats were strongly guarded by soldiers and manned by slaves as rowers. Traders and their *engagées* usually accompanied the convoy,.taking advantage of the opportunity for better protection for their outfits.[106] The frequent attacks made upon the convoy by the Chickasaw and the Cherokee caused heavy losses. Vaudreuil had proposed in 1744 that the convoy be sent up later in the season,[107] to avoid fatigues of heat and dangers from the savages who would cause less trouble in winter days,[108] but nothing seems to have been done about it.

The abuses in connection with the convoy were sometimes so flagrant as to cause investigation even in Louisiana. The convoy which left in August, 1749, under the command of Lieutenant de Montchervaux, was on November 1 still eighty leagues from the Illinois. The slow progress was said to have been due to drunkenness and other disorders on the part of the men, caused by a general lack of discipline. M. de Montcher-

---

[103]The system in Canada required that bills be sent down to the intendant, who often slashed them considerably, whether from actual desire to lower expenses or from other motives. Vaudreuil argued the lack of a rule or regulation to establish a basis for validation. See Vaudreuil and Le Normand to Minister Jan. 4, 1745, *Arch. Nat., Col.*, C¹³A, 29:8ᵛ-9. The minister claimed the chief trouble was due to the greed of the officers at the posts, and to their failure to punish those guilty of speculation. He recommended taking the trade out of their hands and farming out the posts or putting the trade on the license system as was done in Canada. He asked for a report on this. Minister to Vaudreuil and Michel, Versailles, Sept. 26, 1750, *Ibid.*, B, 91:11-11ᵛ.
[104]Minister to Vaudreuil, Versailles, *Ibid.*, B, 83:10ᵛ.
[105]Minister to Vaudreuil and Le Normand, Versailles, Oct. 9, 1747, *Ibid.*, B, 85:14-14ᵛ.
[106]For a description of a convoy going to the Illinois, see Journal of Antoine Bonnefoy, in Mereness, *Travels in the American Colonies*, 241 ff.
[107]He had sent it that year in January because of lack of goods, which had forced a long delay. The usual time of departure was in August, the convoy ordinarily reaching its destination in November. The returning convoy usually left the Illinois in April of the following year, only fifteen days being required for the return trip.
[108]Vaudreuil to Minister, New Orleans, *Arch. Nat., Col.*, C¹³A, 28:249.

vaux submitted a bill of 1,200 livres for a hunter who furnished game for his table! It was also charged that the lieutenant had purposely left the Indian presents behind at New Orleans, buying others for an exorbitant price at La Pointe Coupée. M. Michel called the convoy *"un pillage et une vollerie perpetuelle."*[109] This investigation led in 1750 to the approval of a scheme to send up the king's goods under contract with private individuals.[110] At the same time an order for the trial and punishment of the officer was given. The example of M. de Montchervaux was not unusual in Louisiana where government expenditures were long the chief source of income for the people.[111]

In Canada, as in Louisiana, paper was almost the only circulating medium—and Canada, unlike Louisiana, was not put on a metallic currency at any time during this period. Kalm says: "They have in Canada scarce any other but paper-currency. I hardly ever saw any coin, except French sols, consisting of brass, with a very small mixture of silver; they were quite thin by constant circulation, and were valued at a sol and a half."[112] No coin seems to have been issued for Canada after 1721, when 150,000 marks of copper pieces were ordered.[113] Card money authorizations under the ordinance of May 12, 1733, stood at 600,000 livres.[114] In 1742 this was increased by 120,000 livres.[115] This inflation gave very little relief, most of this amount having been used to retire bills issued in the previous year. Toward the end of the same year Hocquart says he was faced with expenses of 491,000 livres and had on hand only 142,000 livres of card money and 80,000 livres in letters of exchange.[116] It was found necessary to revalue the "old sols" in this period. In 1743 it had been ordered that only a fortieth part of the payment of a bill could be made in this money due to its exaggerated value, and a year later it was ordered that metal sols were no longer to be received except at the value of 18 deniers.[117] At the end of the decade, it was ordered that the circulation of card money should be increased to 1,000,000 livres.[118] There also circulated small amounts of French and foreign coinage, as well as the bills of the intendant (usually retired within a year), and bills of the Company of the Indies.

Attempts were being made at this time to devise a revenue for Canada.

---
[109]M. Michel to Minister, New Orleans, Jan. 22, 1750, *Ibid.*, C¹³A, 34:291-296. Honoré Michel de la Rouvillière, Sieur de Villebois (1737?-1752), was intendant of Louisiana, 1748-1752.
[110]Minister to M. Michel, Versailles, Sept. 26, 1750, *Ibid.*, B, 91:8; also Minister to Vaudreuil and Michel, Versailles, Sept. 26, 1750, *Ibid.*, B, 91:13-13ᵛ. Though the plan to put the convoy under private contract was approved, it was not put into effect.
[111]See "A Chapter of Colonial History," in *La. Hist. Quart.*, VI, 4, 566.
[112]Kalm, *op. cit.*, III, 68-70.
[113]*Edits, Ordonnances*, I, 437.
[114]*Ibid.*, 544-545.
[115]Minister to Hocquart, Feb. 27, 1742, *Can. Arch. Rep.*, 1904, 299; Beauharnois to Minister, Quebec, Sept. 20, 1742, *Arch. Nat., Col.*, C¹¹A, 77:106-107; Hocquart to Minister, Quebec, Apr. 30, 1742, *Ibid.*, C¹¹A, 78:97-105ᵛ.
[116]Hocquart to Minister, Quebec, Oct. 30, 1742, *Ibid.*, C¹¹A, 78:97-105.
[117]*Edits, Ordonnances*, II, 387-388.
[118]Minister to La Galissonière and Bigot, Apr. 18, 1749, *Can. Arch. Rep.*, 1905, I, 112.

In 1733 the king had submitted two schemes for the consideration of the governor and intendant. One of these involved a three per cent tax on exports and imports, the other a *taille* on the inhabitants. Nothing seems to have been done about this, however, and in 1742, the king again referred to the matter by asking for an investigation. He recommended that the *taille* be chosen. For the time being, however, he was content with a small tax on *eau de vie* and wine used for the trade with the Indians (3-4 livres per barrel on brandy, and 4 sols per pot on wines).[119] A special duty on wines, *eau de vie,* and rum was levied to contribute toward the expense of building the fortifications of Quebec. In 1747 these duties were augmented for a three-year period as follows:[120]

	Old Duty	New Duty
Wine, hogshead	9 livres	12 livres
Eau de vie, velt (7 qt.)	16 sols, 8 deniers	1 livre, 4 sols
Rum, hogshead	15 livres	24 livres

In February, 1748, an edict was issued placing a three per cent tariff on all goods entering or leaving Canada, excepting wines, brandies, and rums taxed under the *Ordonnance* of 1747. Additional exceptions were made in the case of food exports to the islands or other French colonies, goods outgoing and ingoing for Canadian fisheries, as well as on cordage, salt, horses, new ships built in Canada, salt herring, and a few others. Elk skins going out were also exempted, because they had been previously taxed.[121] It was provided, however, that this edict was not to go into effect until the end of the war.[122] Sometimes levies were made on the *bourgeoisie;* one in Montreal in 1741 amounted to 5,000 livres.[123]

Administrative expenses of Canada averaged slightly over 100,000 livres per year. The recapitulation for 1741 is as follows:[124]

	Livres
Appointments of officials, and entertainment of special garrisons	23,250
Religious Houses	57,200
Officers of Justice	11,330
Hospital of Quebec	1,600
Extraordinary expenses	1,800
Expenses of Isle Royale	15,750
Expenses of sending a Doctor of Botany to Louisiana	2,000
Total	112,930

[119] Memoir of the King to Beauharnois and Hocquart, Fontainebleau, Apr. 30, 1742, *Arch. Nat., Col.,* B, 74:503-511. In general the colonial trade was regulated by the edict of May 12, 1717. Under this edict colonial products were to be received into France free of any duties excepting the farmer general's (of revenue) tax. Goods destined for other countries from French colonies were to be transshipped from French ports. The tax on hides, for example, was 5 sols each. In general this duty on colonial imports was three per cent *ad valorem.* An export duty on colonial goods transshipped to foreign ports was also levied. Naturally the whole trade was regulated strictly in accordance with the demands of the mercantilist system. *Recueuils de Règlemens, Edits, Declarations et Arrêts,* etc., 46-61.
[120] *Edits, Ordonnances,* Jan. 23, 1747, I, 589.
[121] *Ibid.,* I, 591-594. For table of duties on specific articles, see *Ibid.,* 594 ff.
[122] *Ibid.,* 608-609.
[123] *Bordereau,* 1741, *Arch. Nat., Col.,* C¹¹A, 114:336-402ᵛ.
[124] *Ibid.,* C¹¹A, 115:10-13. For the year 1742, the same was 116,430 livres. *Ibid.,* C¹¹A, 115: 27-31. Other examples of this administrative expense are: 1747, 103,250 livres, *Ibid.,* C¹¹A, 115: 381-382ᵛ; 1746, 105,680 livres, *Ibid.,* C¹¹A, 115:301-302; 1745, 115,080 livres, *Ibid.,* C¹¹A, 115:146-150ᵛ.

In this same year, the *bordereau* shows the following figures:[125]

	Livres	Sols	Deniers
Funds ordained in the king's statement, May 14, 1741...	358,248	16	4
From which deduct excedents of previous year..........	34,623	16	4
Which leaves...	323,625	...	..
Plus extraordinary receipts, bringing it up to...........	412,458	4	8
Total expenses, all deductions made...................	515,627	19	6
Excedents of expenses on receipts.....................	103,169	14	10

In 1744, the king allowed about the same amount (386,173 livres, 13 sols, 7 deniers), while deductions for previous excesses amounted to 53,623 livres, 3 sols, 7 deniers, leaving 332,550 livres, 10 sols, to which of course was to be added extraordinary receipts and the income from the fur trade.[126] Again, in 1745, the king allowed 491,517 livres, 15 sols, 4 deniers, but deductions for excesses amounted to 161,163 livres, 2 sols, 10 deniers, this due to the increase of extraordinary expenses by reason of the war with the English.[127] During the war, of course, expenses mounted wildly in Canada on account of the huge outlays that were made.[128]

Many other items of expenditure in Canada were not usually charged to the colony's account. These included a sum of over 100,000 livres yearly for the maintenance of the king's domain,[129] and such outlays as those for shipbuilding at Quebec, the operation of the forges at St. Maurice, and others.

There was regularly allowed for acquittals of extraordinary expenses in Canada 250,000 livres authorized in letters of exchange in addition to the amounts granted as the stocks for the king's stores. This item we may be sure was regularly exceeded. In 1739 the total of letters of exchange issued amounted to 280,401 livres, an excess of 30,401 livres over the authorization. This, of course, was an abnormal year due to heavy consumptions in raising and equipping the army which was to be sent against the Chickasaw, though this expenditure was finally charged to Louisiana's account. We may assume that this item grew larger during the heavier expenditures of the war of 1744-1748.[130]

The greater part of excesses in expenses was due to the extraordinary expenses incurred at the several posts of the colony. These outlays were for the maintenance of the service in various ways: chiefly in payment of freight and shipping charges, expenses for errands and voyages, and considerable outlays for the savages in food, merchandise, repairing of arms, and so forth. Outlays to the Indians were made either as presents for obtaining their good will, or for subsidizing their war parties, as

---

[125]*Bordereau*, 1741, *Ibid.*, C¹¹A, 114:336-402ᵛ.
[126]*Arch. Nat., Col.*, C¹¹A, 115:65. It should be noted that the revenues from the fur trade gave Canada a considerable sum, which was not true in Louisiana.
[127]*Ibid.*, C¹¹A, 115:150.
[128]See *infra*, pp. 32 ff.
[129]Minister to Beauharnois and Hocquart, June 19, 1745, *Ibid.*, B, 81:314ᵛ.
[130]Minister to Hocquart, Versailles, Apr. 24, 1740, *Ibid.*, B, 70:333-333ᵛ.

well as for relief to them in times of scarcity.[131] At times extraordinary expenses were occasioned also for the entertainment of the garrison of the post itself, when the king's stores had been depleted of their stocks. These needs were supplied by purchases from traders at the posts, generally at high prices, for costs of freight alone from, say Detroit to Montreal, were estimated at thirty per cent of the value of the goods. Then, too, there was much dishonest dealing carried on.

Upon delivery of goods, or shortly thereafter, a certificate was drawn up by the commandant of the post and the trader, which gave a detailed list of the goods furnished, with quantities and prices of each item as well as the total amount. This certificate was signed by the trader and the post commandant as an evidence of its verity. The certificate then went to the intendant and governor who passed upon it, the intendant scaling down individual figures or the total sum as he saw fit.[132] It was then acquitted by a letter of exchange, by card money, or by a bill issued by the intendant. A copy of the bill was made by the commissary where it was acquitted (in case of the western posts this was done at Montreal), and this copy was sent to the minister along with the general *bordereau* of expense.

The policy was to separate administrative expenses of the posts from other expenses. These were supposed to be paid by the proceeds from licenses to traders. Administrative expenses included such items as gratifications of officers detached, of the missionary, of the interpreter, of the surgeon, and of the almoner, but not the pay of the garrison, if any. Officers were usually forbidden to keep their wives at the posts, in order to cut down expense, and allowances for storekeepers and other help were minimized.[133] Abuses on the part of the storekeepers were not uncommon, and were much complained of,[134] the officers themselves being sometimes implicated.[135]

---

[131] Hocquart to Minister, Oct. 14, 1742, *Ibid.*, C11A, 78:28-34v.

[132] The expense bills for the western posts are found in the *Archives Nationales, Colonies*, at Paris. The C11A series, vol. 117, contains most of the bills for the period under consideration. No expense bills for the Louisiana posts have been preserved. This material, which has persistently been neglected by scholars in the past, has been used in the preparation of this dissertation as one of the chief sources. Its value lies in the fact that it contains details that are most often missing in other documents. For a record of movements of the French and savages at the posts it is invaluable. In the field of prices and trading activity it is also very useful. Great care must be taken, however, to guard against deceptions of many kinds, for it should be remembered that though these bills were subject to the censorship of the intendant, he was also subject to peculation. Pouchot says many "hypothecated accounts" were turned in, especially during war. *Memoir on the Late War*, II, 50-51. Sometimes the "moderations" of the intendant were drastic, either upon the excuse that prices charged were too high, or else when the amounts specified to have been furnished were in doubt. Doubtless other reasons of less justifiable nature may sometimes have influenced the intendant to make a reduction. An example of most drastic reduction is found in the case of a bill of furnishings at the store of Sieur Charly at the Post of the Miamis in December, 1744. In this instance Hocquart moderated a bill for 1491 livres to 100 livres. *Arch. Nat., Col.*, C11A, 82:213. On the other hand, Hocquart signed a bill in favor of the Sieur Gamelin at the Wea post in June, 1746, which allowed thirty per cent carrying charges on the bill. *Ibid.*, C11A, 85:287-290.

[133] Minister to Hocquart, Fontainebleau, Apr. 20, 1742, *Arch. Nat., Col.*, B, 74:478-478v.

[134] See discussion of the case of La Force at Niagara, in Hocquart to Minister, October 26, 1740, *Ibid.*, C11A, 73:306-309.

[135] See accusations against the Sieur Dupiessis-Fabert, commandant at Michilimakinac, for fraud in purchases of his brandy supply. Minister to La Jonquière, Versailles, May 31, 1750, *Wisc. Hist. Coll.*, XVIII, 61-62; also La Jonquière to Minister, Quebec, Sept. 20, 1750, *Ibid.*, 67.

It would appear that the income from trading licenses at the posts was usually sufficient to meet ordinary expenses of administration, even though the king often deducted certain sums for poor relief from the income from trading permits. Consider the case of Detroit individually for 1742. M. de Céloron reports that in that year, the income from licenses at his post was 6,000 livres. The outlays against this were 3,000 livres for the commandant's gratuity, 621 livres, 10 sols, for expenses of a certain trip he had made (it would appear this might have been charged to extraordinary expenses), 500 livres to the almoner, 300 livres to the surgeon, and 400 livres to the interpreter, which left 1,178 livres, 10 sols, which he had used to pay for supplies and for other uses at the post.[136]

Receipts necessarily varied with the years. In 1743, a normal year, total receipts from *congés* and farms of the posts of the upper country amounted to 47,783 livres. After all charges against this had been paid, amounting to 38,682 livres, a surplus of 9,101 livres was remitted to the treasury.[137] The statements for the years 1745 and 1746 are not at hand, but they doubtless showed a lean harvest due to the war and resulting unsettled conditions in the upper country,[138] for as early as 1744 the receipts amounted to only 17,661 livres.[139] However, receipts for 1747, a year which saw the Indian uprising in the upper country, are 46,600 livres, or 10,452 livres above all expenses. Part of this large sum of receipts is to be explained in the fact that the accounts show collection of several installments of back dues on the rent of farms. The next year receipts amounted to 31,868 livres, 13 sols, 6 deniers, and expenses were 26,134 livres, 7 sols, leaving a surplus of 5,734 livres, 6 sols, 6 deniers.[140] These samples reveal that the administrative expenses of the Canadian posts were easily met by the proceeds of the fur trade, possibly even in the worst years, though the material at hand does not allow an exact account of this.

With extraordinary expense, however, it is different. The regular incomes were, of course, very inadequate to meet the strain of war or unusual expenses such as those incurred at the instance of the Indian revolt in the upper country in 1747. In 1744 at the beginning of the English war, we find that over 100,000 livres were required to stock the king's stores "at the occasion of the war," that is, to put them in con-

---

[136] Beauharnois to Minister, Quebec, Nov. 2, 1742, *Mich. Pion. and Hist. Coll.* (Cadillac Papers), 34, 211.
[137] Included in expenditures were bills of 12,232 livres for the relief of Canadian poor, 6,250 livres for the Montreal fortifications, and 2,000 livres for the establishment of the Algonkin and Nepissing at Lake of the Two Mountains. *Arch. Nat., Col.,* C¹¹A, 115:32-33ᵛ.
[138] A study of the record of *congés* shows that in 1745 there were forty-three *congés* issued for the trade, which was ten less than the fifty-three issued in 1743. In 1746 the number fell still lower, to thirty-two. Detroit, for instance, got only eight in 1745, while she had fourteen in the previous year. The falling off in the number of *congés* of course lessened the income, while many of the farmers failed in their rents also.
[139] *Arch. Nat., Col.,* C¹¹A, 115:65-65ᵛ.
[140] Report of La Galissonière, Sept. 29, 1749, *Ibid.,* C¹¹A, 116:144 ff. This report covers the years 1747 and 1748 and gives an estimation of the incomes and expenses for 1749.

dition for war issues on a somewhat adequate scale.[141] In 1746, when the war effort was at its highest, incident to the threatened English campaign against Canada from New York, the total issues from the stores of Montreal and Quebec amounted to over 1,000,000 livres,[142] and in the first eight months of the next year, Montreal expended for various war parties against New England over 335,000 livres.[143] Nearly 100,000 livres of this amount was spent for one expedition, which netted only a few scalps.[144] Due to these heavy expenditures which served only to aggravate the ills of the French treasury, the king decided to put the colony on a defensive basis in 1748, abandoning offensive tactics.[145] The fact that negotiations for peace were then being held may be another factor in the issuing of this order.

Expenses for Indian administration may be put into two categories: expenses for incidental movements and general oversight of the Indians at the posts, and outlays for presents. Presents were usually distributed at Montreal and Quebec, though post commanders and special messengers also made presents in certain cases. Of course much greater outlays were made to the Indians for war purposes and, in cases of emergency, for their support. In regard to the first item we find that only 5,000 livres were expended in 1740-1741.[146] On the other hand, outlays for presents were far greater, amounting in 1741, a normal year, to about 65,000 livres. Part of this sum was, however, of an unusual nature, for in this year Beauharnois attempted to move the Huron from Detroit to Montreal. The expenses of this venture amounted to more than a fourth part of the 48,000 livres laid out to the Indians of Montreal that year.[147] When it is considered that the inventories of all the king's stores excepting only that at Fort Frontenac showed only 232,545 livres, 8 sols, 8 deniers, this outlay appears all the more considerable. In 1744 Indian presents were slightly in excess of 60,000 livres,[148] this being the first war year, while administrative expenses rose to over 10,000 livres for the western Indians in 1745.[149] It might seem strange that the total expended for presents shows a decline in 1746 and 1747. In the former year, for instance, the total for presents is given as 41,634 livres, 4 sols, 4 deniers,[150] while that for 1747, the year of the Indian rebellion in the upper country, was put at 33,391 livres, 7 sols, 8 deniers.[151] This is explained in the fact that

---
[141]Hocquart to Minister, Quebec, Oct. 29, 1744, Ibid., C¹¹A, 82:159-159ᵛ.
[142]Ibid., C¹¹A, 117:48.
[143]Ibid., C¹¹A, 117:320ᵛ.
[144]Ibid., C¹¹A, 117:20-31.
[145]Minister to La Galissonière, Mar. 6, 1748, Can. Arch. Rep., 1905, 1, 105.
[146]See Hocquart to Minister, Quebec, Nov. 3, 1740, Arch. Nat., Col., C¹¹A, 73:381-383; Bordereau, 1741, Ibid., C¹¹A, 114:392-392ᵛ.
[147]Hocquart to Minister, Quebec, Oct. 24, 1741, Ibid., C¹¹A, 76:14-17ᵛ.
[148]Minister to Hocquart, March 31, 1745, Can. Arch. Rep., 1905, 1, 40.
[149]Hocquart to Minister, Quebec, Nov. 2, 1745, Arch. Nat., Col., C¹¹A, 84:106ᵛ-107.
[150]Ibid., C¹¹A, 117:91-93.
[151]Ibid., C¹¹A, 117:144-146. Outlays made at the western posts were, of course, much higher in these years, the expense accounts showing the greatest outlays in extraordinary expense

most Indians allied to the French were in Montreal in those years engaged in the war with the English. They were of course supported here under regular war issues. Since most of these warriors brought their families with them, extraordinary outlays for the war itself were greatly increased. Indian refugees from the east also gathered at Montreal and Quebec to be supported on the government's dole. We find the governor and intendant hard put to defend these large outlays.[152] Of course, there were the usual outlays for presents for diplomatic purposes.[153]

Canada also made in these years considerable outlays for the Chickasaw War. The campaign of 1739-1740 cost 136,857 livres, 11 sols, 9 deniers, though this amount was eventually charged to the account of Louisiana.[154] Minor outlays were made for the continuance of the war, chiefly in the years 1741-1743.[155]

The expenditures of the colony for religious and charitable purposes have been discussed above. Some of the larger outlays for the church and religion were 12,700 livres for the support of the bishop and cathedral at Quebec, 7,600 livres for the support of the country *curés*, and 9,000 livres to the Jesuits for their missions both in the west and in the east (Abenaki missions). The Seminary of the Sulpicians at Montreal got 6,000 livres, and the various other organizations got smaller amounts. The total of this item in 1741 was 57,200 livres, and it remained about the same every year.[156] Each year 10,000 livres or more went to poor relief for the whites.[157]

---

in the decade. Not counting the Illinois (for which expense accounts are not extant in the Paris Archives), we find that the total outlay at the posts in the year 1746 was 17,796 livres, 10 sols, 11 deniers, and in 1747 it had soared to 50,159 livres, 7 sols, 8 deniers. The chief cause of the unusual expenditure was, of course, the Indian rebellion, but it is impossible to tell with certainty how much went to this item and how much went to other accounts. In any case, the fact that the outlay for 1747 was nearly half of the total outlays for this item for the years 1740-1748 is significant. The chief posts affected by the insurrection naturally made the greatest outlays, though it happened that these two posts, Detroit and Michilimakinac, were also the greatest trading centers, and hence there was more material to be bought at those posts. The latter post in 1746 had bills totalling more than 6,000 livres, which was at least one-third larger than the same item for the previous year. In 1747, her bills totalled more than 20,000 livres, this being by far the largest expenditure of any post for this item. Detroit, having practically no outlay for this item in 1746, expended over 8,000 livres in the following year. Most of these expenses were laid out in purchases of powder, lead, and food for the savages. Large amounts were also laid out in connection with numerous conferences with the Indians, especially in distributing presents to those of undoubted loyalty. Of course, Montreal had large expenses in these years in sending up armed forces with the trading convoys going up to the posts.
[152]Beauharnois to Minister, Oct. 13, 1743, *Wisc. Hist. Coll.*, XVII, 439; see also *Doc. Rel. to the Col. Hist. of N. Y.*, IX, 1095 ff.
[153]In 1746 Hocquart said he had been feeding at Quebec alone throughout the winter from 700 to 800 Indians. Hocquart to Minister, Quebec, Sept. 18, 1746, *Arch. Nat., Col.*, C11A, 85:310-310v. Again the same writer reports that he entertained ninety deputies of the Five Nations at Quebec for two months, which cost over 25,000 livres. La Corne's journey to the upper country in 1746 for the purpose of recruiting Indians for the war cost over 60,000 livres. Hocquart to Minister, Sept. 24, 1746, *Ibid.*, C11A, 88:15-19v.
[154]Minister to Hocquart, Marly, April 27, 1741, *Ibid.*, B, 72:369-369v.
[155]In 1741 a bill for 6,000 livres is found for this item. *Ibid.*, C11A, 76:181-185. Totals of extraordinary expense bills for the western posts fell from 15,000 livres in 1740 to less than 5,000 livres in 1741 and about the same in 1742. Most parties sent against the Chickasaw seem to have been sent in these last two years. The total of the bills of 1743 was less than 3,000 livres.
[156]*Ibid.*, C11A, 115:10v-11v.
[157]Memoir of the King to Beauharnois and Hocquart, Versailles, Mar. 24, 1744, *Ibid.*, B, 78:326-327.

Chapter II

POPULATION AND INDUSTRY

THE TOTAL non-Indian population of Louisiana as estimated in 1746 was 8,830.[1] These people were located on the coast from Mobile Bay to New Orleans, and on the Mississippi from New Orleans to the Illinois country. Small settlements were also found on the Missouri, the Wabash, the Red, and the Arkansas rivers. Of this total, 2,500 were men (*habitants,* or soldiers), 1,500 were women and children, and 4,730 were negro slaves of both sexes, including mixed breeds. Most of the white population of Louisiana had originally come from Canada, though some, especially women, had come from France.[2]

New Orleans, the capital city of the province, contained several hundred inhabitants and boasted platted streets and a levee system. At La Pointe Coupée, Les Allemands (the German settlement), and farther up the river at Natchez, were other considerable settlements about which were large farming communities. Each of these places was fortified, New Orleans having forts both near the city and below near the mouth of the river. Other smaller posts with forts were at Natchitoches on the Red River, Fort Tombechbee on the river of that name, and the Alabama fort on the Alabama River. These minor posts usually consisted of a small log fort surrounded with a palisade with four bastions. A store house and traders' quarters comprised the rest of the "post." A small cannon or two with a few mortars made up the artillery. On war footing such a post might be manned by twenty to forty men with a few officers.

A short distance above the mouth of the Arkansas River was located Arkansas Post. This establishment was the second oldest in Louisiana, and had been the center of Law's colonizing activities, but it was now reduced to a small garrison post of twenty soldiers or fewer. Near the fort were established a dozen *habitants,* with possibly as many slaves. They busied themselves with hunting the buffalo and bear, the meat of which they salted and sent down the river to the settlements below or sold in part to the garrison at the post. This place was noted for its bears' oil, which served as a substitute for butter in the western country. A small amount of tobacco was also raised, the surplus being sold to the traders or to the savages. In 1749, after a raid by the Chickasaw, the post was moved from the river bank some distance inland so as to secure the protection of the Arkansas Indians who lived nearby.[3]

---

[1]Memoir on Louisiana, 1746, *Arch. Nat., Col.,* C¹³A, 30:256-257.
[2]Le Page Du Pratz, *Histoire de La Louisiane,* II, 299-300; Memoir on Louisiana, 1746, *Arch. Nat., Col.,* C¹³A, 30:271.
[3]For a description of the Arkansas post, see Memoir on Louisiana, 1746, *Arch. Nat., Col.,* C¹³A, 30:250; Le Page Du Pratz, *op. cit.,* 290-291; Le Mascrier's *Dumont,* II, 68. Dumont

Fort Prudhomme had been built on the Memphis Bluffs in 1682, and rebuilt as Fort L'Assomption in 1739 during Bienville's Chickasaw campaign. However, this place along with a small post at the mouth of the St. Francis River had been destroyed by Bienville in 1740. The next settlements were those in the Illinois country, where there were located five villages, containing in all at least a thousand French and half as many negroes.[4] There was also a small settlement on the Missouri River, about ninety leagues from its mouth, containing perhaps a score of *habitants* who owned half as many slaves. Some corn was raised here, but the people were chiefly engaged in hunting and trading. A small settlement was also located on the Wabash at the site of Vincennes, where, it was estimated in 1746, there were forty *habitants* and five negroes engaged in raising corn and tobacco.[5]

The government was aware of the need for more settlers, but seems to have depended largely upon the natural increase rather than immigration. Settlers once located in Louisiana were rarely allowed to leave because of fear of weakening the colony by the loss of numbers. It should be mentioned that colonists often would gladly have returned to the homeland, and allowing some to leave would only have served to increase the discontentment of those remaining.[6] The importation of slaves was minimized, only one shipload coming in during the decade of the 1740's. This was due to the fact that the number of slaves was already very high in proportion to the white population.[7] Early marriages were encouraged, the minimum ages of eighteen for men and fourteen for women having been fixed in 1748. At this time also, some additional settlers were being sent over from France, these being composed chiefly of convicted salt smugglers.[8]

Canada was, of course, much more populous than Louisiana. A census was ordered to be taken in 1745, but the result is not found among the documents.[9] A note on Pouchot's manuscript refers to a census taken about 1750 which places the total population at 88,000.[10] Most of the

---

says there was no fort there but only a little "corps de garde" and store house. For plans of the Tombechbee fort, see the *Dumont Ms.*, 256. See also testimony of one Lantinac, French deserter, on the Alabama forts, in *South Carolina Council Minutes*, Apr. 14, 1747, 80-82, *Public Record Office, Colonial Office*, 5, v. 455. The same authority gives the population of New Orleans as 500, including fifty soldiers stationed at the fort, while the male population of Mobile was estimated at one hundred, exclusive of three companies of soldiers.

[4] The memoir of 1746 cited above puts the number of *habitants* as 200-300, both figures being used in different statements. The number of black slaves is put at 600. Father Vivier gives the total number of whites as 1,100, and that of slaves as 360, including both red and black. Father Vivier to Father ———, June 8, 1750, Thwaites, *Jes. Rel.*, 69, 145-147. The Illinois villages were Kaskaskia, Prairie du Rocher, St. Philippe, and the Cahokia village. Some few *habitants* were located near Fort Chartres, and at Sainte Genevieve, on the Missouri side.

[5] Memoir on Louisiana in 1746, *Arch. Nat., Col.*, C¹³A, 30:252.

[6] Minister to Bienville, Jan. 19, 1742, Versailles, *Ibid.*, B, 74:622-623ᵛ. Bienville had requested that settlers from Martinique be allowed to come to Louisiana, paying for their passage with slaves or goods, but the minister seems to have disapproved of this proposition.

[7] *Ibid.*

[8] Memoir of the King for Instruction to M. Michel, Dec. 9, 1748, *Ibid.*, B, 87:28-28ᵛ.

[9] *Edits, Ordonnances*, II, 390.

[10] It is interesting to note, however, that Pouchot erroneously put it at 30,000. Pouchot, *Memoir on the Late War*, II, 45.

Canadian population was centered at Quebec and Montreal, with smaller settlements along the river between these points.

Of the western settlements, Detroit was the most considerable, having a population of about 1,500 French, according to one estimation, though this seems somewhat high.[11] There were said to be as many farmers there as traders, but the chief business was always the fur trade, which De Noyan, the commandant, estimated in 1742 as being worth 150,000-200,000 livres yearly.[12] The same writer tells us that Montreal merchants held more mortgages on Detroit property than the whole town was worth. In addition there was a considerable French settlement at Michilimakinac, which also had a large fur trade, but we have no estimation of the number of people there. A small number of inhabitants was also found near each of the posts of River St. Joseph, the Miami, and the Wea.[13] It is doubtful if more than a very few were located at any of these, the same being true of *La Baye* located at Green Bay on Lake Michigan. The more remote posts such as Chequamigon and La Vérendrye's posts were merely trading stations.

The houses of the western settlers were very simple in construction, being usually built of notched logs, or else of upright timbers set in the ground. The cracks were stopped with clay and sticks to keep out the cold. The floor was commonly made of dirt, though sometimes wood or stone was used. For heating and cooking there was the fireplace with a stone hearth. There was no glass for the windows, and the roof was usually of wooden shingles or "clap-boards" fastened on with wooden pins.[14] The more wealthy inhabitants built their houses of hewn timbers or of stone. The interiors were usually plastered or "white-washed" with lime. Furniture was scarce and commonly hand-made.[15]

Women outnumbered men in Canada, especially in the east, though the reverse was true in the western settlements. We have seen that men far outnumbered women in the whole of Louisiana. Kalm says: "They told me, that they reckon four women to one man in Canada, because annually several Frenchmen are killed in their expeditions, which they undertake for the sake of trading with the Indians."[16] Pouchot gives a

---

[11]Memoir on Louisiana in 1746, *Arch. Nat., Col., C¹¹A*, 30.270. De Noyan placed the number at one hundred resident families. This does not count the large floating population of traders. De Noyan to Minister, Detroit, Aug. 6, 1740, *Wisc. Hist. Coll.*, XVII, 326-327.
[12]See chapter on Fur Trade, below.
[13]These posts were located near the present towns of Niles, Michigan, Ft. Wayne, Indiana, and Lafayette, Indiana, respectively.
[14]Nails were very scarce in the western country, though they are mentioned at times. In the expense bill drawn at De Noyelle's order at Michilimakinac, Apr. 22, 1747, and furnished by M. Janisse we note the following: "500 nails @ 8 l. per C. -40 l." *Arch. Nat., Col.*, C¹¹A, 117:345. Also in a bill of June 19, 1747, furnished by Rupellais de Gonnéville we find this item: "500 roofing nails @ 7 l./C. -35 l." *Ibid.*, C¹¹A, 117:400. These are the only instances of nails mentioned in the expense accounts of Michilimakinac. Nails are also mentioned in the Account Book of the Detroit Mission, Thwaites, *Jes. Rel.*, 69, 245-253. Note the following account: "I owe françois Campeau 500 large nails, at 45 sols A hundred. I owe the same 800 shingle-nails, at 10 sols a hundred; also 200 shingle-nails, at 20 sols A hundred; . . . . and 300 large and 100 medium-sized nails." p. 249.
[15]The description of houses given above is based on Pouchot's account of houses at Niagara, vol. I, 52-53, and Kalm's account of houses of the habitants at Ft. St. Frederic, *op. cit.*, II, 14.
[16]Kalm, *op. cit.*, III, 41-42.

favorable account of the deference paid to women by men. He described the women as being modest, of comely figure, vivacious in spirit, and full of intrigue. "It is only through them that their husbands procure employment . . . ."[17] Neither of these observers failed to mention the good manners of the women, as well as their ability to dance. As to their dress, Kalm observes that they always wore their hair "curled and powdered and ornamented with glittering bodkins and aigrettes. Every day but Sunday they wear a little neat jacket, and a short petticoat which hardly reaches half the leg, and in this particular they seem to imitate the *Indian* women. The heels of their shoes are high, and very narrow, and it is surprising how they walk on them . . . . "

As to their prowess as housekeepers, however, he was not so full of praise, noticing that they were "rather remiss in regard to the cleaning of the utensils, and apartments, for sometimes the floors, both in town and country, were hardly cleaned once in six months, which is a disagreeable sight to one who comes from amongst the *Dutch* and English, where the constant scouring and scrubbing of floors, is reckoned as important as the exercise of religion itself." He said that rather than sweep the floor, they were in the habit of wetting it with water to keep down the dust.[18] Though this description is of the homes of the people in eastern Canada, it would doubtless apply to the people and homes of the western country as well, especially in the older settlements such as the Illinois. The men dressed much after the Indian fashion, wearing trousers and moccasins of deerskin, a cloth shirt, and the Mackinaw blanket, or *capot,* about the shoulders in cold weather.

In the western outposts, the food of the whites was the same as that of the natives—chiefly fish, game, and Indian corn, though sometimes Illinois flour and bear's grease were added to the diet. Liquor was used freely when it could be had, especially wine and brandy. Kalm says three meals per day were customary. The upper classes used brandy, chocolate, or coffee for breakfast, but no tea. The mid-day meal as described by Kalm consisted of a variety of dishes—fresh meats and salads, wine or spruce beer, wheaten bread, with berries, cheese, or nuts either fresh or preserved for dessert. On fast days fish, eggs, and milk prepared in various ways were used. He says both the French and English used much less sugar than his own pople (the Swedes). The evening meal was said to be practically the same as the noon-day meal. The country people, according to Kalm, contented themselves with eating bread, and saving their poultry, eggs, butter, cheese, and flesh, for sale in the towns, the proceeds from which were used to buy liquor and clothing.[19]

---
[17]Pouchot, *op. cit.*, II, 45-46.
[18]Kalm, *op. cit.*, III, 55-57.
[19]*Ibid.,* 184 ff. In another place, he says the poor people ate onions almost universally, and that the use of tobacco was just as common. In my study of the expense accounts I have

POPULATION AND INDUSTRY 39

The health of the people in Louisiana was none too good, according to the information available. During this period, smallpox, mumps, and "la grippe" were prevalent in the whole colony of Louisiana. Smallpox was brought over with a shipload of slaves in 1743, and though not as deadly as the epidemic of 1734, it was nevertheless a serious plague. As to mumps, it was thought to have come in with some soldiers in 1740, while "la grippe" is thought to have come from the Illinois. Many people died of the latter, according to one report. Children during this time were said to have been afflicted with a serious disease of the gums.[20] In 1749 Vaudreuil reported that an epidemic of sickness had raged in the Illinois for two years and had so seriously affected the inhabitants as to be responsible for the small wheat crops in that region during those years.[21] It will be seen that in the Chickasaw campaign of 1739-1740 sickness among Bienville's troops was blamed in part for the poor showing made against the enemy.[22]

As to the health of the Canadians, Pouchot described them as a hardy and robust people.[23] Kalm observes, however, that Frenchmen born in France were said to live longer than those born in Canada. He was also told that they could do more work and stand more hardships than the Canadian-born French. Rheumatism and "pleurisies" were common among both the Canadians and the Indians. Venereal disease was very common, and worms were found, according to Kalm, more often in Canada than in the New England colonies. Fevers, however, were less common, though "ship-fever" was often brought in.[24]

In general, the people seem to have been of loose morals, though devoted to the church and their religion. The traders and *coureurs de bois* were perhaps the worst element, though the church attempted to hold them to account when they were in the civilized communities.[25] In the Illinois, Father Vivier was poorly impressed with the religious devotion of the French, especially of those who were traders in *eau de vie* at his mission.[26] Kalm says the French were certainly more devout than the English. Besides having morning and evening prayer on the ships as the English did, he said they had extra prayers on Sundays which the English did not have. At Fort St. Frederic all soldiers were gathered for morning and

---

never seen listed any foodstuffs excepting corn, flour, game, meat, and bear's grease. Of course, tobacco, wine, and brandy were common. It is true that most of these issues were made to savages, but many were also made for use in post garrisons. Dairy products, vegetables, fruits, and the like must have been supplied by the farms, especially at Detroit, Michilimakinac, and the Illinois.

[20]"A Chapter in Colonial History," *La. Hist. Quart.*, VI, 4, 567.
[21]Vaudreuil to Minister, Aug. 26, 1749, *Arch. Nat., Col.*, C¹³A, 33:58.
[22]For an account of this campaign and its difficulties, see Caldwell, Norman W., "The Chickasaw Threat to French Control of the Mississippi in the 1740's," *Chronicles of Oklahoma*, XVI, No. 4 (December, 1938), 465-492.
[23]Pouchot, *op. cit.*, II, 45.
[24]Kalm, *op. cit.*, III, 8-9, 32-34.
[25]Pouchot, *op. cit.*, II, 46.
[26]Father Vivier to Father ———, Nov. 17, 1750, Thwaites, *Jes. Rel.*, 69, 200-203.

evening prayer.[27] We have seen that the Recollets regularly ministered to the army.

Agriculture in the west may be studied best in the Illinois country. In 1716, the king had issued an edict redistributing lands held by private individuals, with the end in view of forcing landholders to give more attention to the cultivation of their lands. Large concessions formerly granted were to be reduced in size, and the timber reserves left to the *concessionaires* were to be limited to their actual needs. The lands so recovered were to be regranted in plots of two to four *arpents* of frontage by forty to sixty in depth. Each new concession was to be held in free tenure by the individual or his heirs, provided also that the *concessionaire* should agree to submit to any *seigneurial* rights that might in the future be established. An individual could sell land only after he had cultivated at least two-thirds of it, and the king reserved the right to take any timber needed for the construction of forts, docks, wharves, ships, or other uses.[28] On the basis of this edict, all land grants were made in the decade under consideration.

In the Illinois, most of the concessions were held under grants made in the time of the Mississippi Company. These were not disturbed except possibly in 1743 when a new common for the pasturage of cattle and horses was established on the peninsula formed by the Kaskaskia and Mississippi rivers. This infringed somewhat upon some existing grants. Cattle and horses were to be kept there in common by the villagers. It was also used as a timber reserve for the use of the people.[29]

If agriculture did not prosper in the Illinois, it was not from lack of verbal encouragement by the royal government. In 1744, the minister pointed out that too much attention was being given to mining and trading, while agriculture was being neglected.[30] De Bertet seemed more interested in development of the mines than in agriculture, an attitude which brought the minister's censure upon him. At the end of the war with the English, plans were made for increasing land cultivation by sending convicted salt smugglers (*faux sauniers*), whom De Bertet had requested for working the mines.[31] In line with this policy to encourage agriculture in the Illinois, Vaudreuil proposed that the further importation of slaves to that region be prohibited. He reported that the large number of slaves there tended to cause the whites to idle and to neglect their work. He admitted, however, that a few might have to be sent up to keep the Illinois *habitants*

---

[27]Kalm, *op. cit.*, III, 43-44.
[28]*La. Hist. Quart.*, XIV, 3, 346-348. The French *arpent* was equal to 192.75 feet, English measure.
[29]*Ordonnance* of Vaudreuil and Salmon, Aug. 14, 1743, in Breese, *op. cit.*, app. F., 294-296. This common was used for breeding and rearing stock. The work stock were kept in a common about the village.
[30]Minister to De Bertet, Versailles, Jan. 1, 1744, *Arch. Nat., Col.*, B, 78:8-8ᵛ.
[31]Minister to De Bertet, Versailles, Dec. 23, 1748, *Ibid.*, B, 87:33-33ᵛ. De Bertet (some put it De Bertel or Berthelot) was commandant in the Illinois from 1742 to 1749, in which year he died.

from raising serious objections in case new slaves should be received in Louisiana.[32] (The only slaves received in the 1740's were the shipload which came over in 1743.)[33] The minister having replied favorably on this subject, the governor and intendant in 1745 forbade negroes to be sent up to the Illinois, a step which was approved a year later by the minister, who then ordered an ordinance to be promulgated on the subject.[34] Accordingly, the importation of slaves into the Illinois was definitely forbidden.

Farming methods were crude. The wooden plow, pulled by oxen, was used to break the ground, while the old style harrow, shaped like an "A," and also of wood, was used to pulverize it. Crude carts took the place of wagons, these also being of wooden construction. Corn and wheat were the chief crops, though oats and hops were also grown. There were also the common fruits and vegetables of France and Canada, such as onions, pumpkins, cabbages, and others. Father Vivier reported that the country produced all crops necessary to life.[35] He says horses, pigs, and cattle were raised in considerable numbers.[36] As to the yield of wheat in the Illinois, Father Vivier said it was only five to eight fold. He charged this to the careless methods of tilling the soil, reporting that some land had been cultivated for thirty years without the use of manure. It was also his opinion that the river fogs and excessive heat damaged the wheat. Corn, however, was said to grow exceedingly well, yielding more than a thousand fold—a figure which seems a bit high, even to those who have had experience in raising corn on rich Mississippi *alluvium*. Indian corn, the food of the savages, was used to feed cattle, hogs, and slaves. Father Vivier estimated that the country produced three times as much food as was consumed there yearly.

Illinois flour as exported to New Orleans and elsewhere represents the best gauge by which to measure the success of agriculture in the Illinois country. The prices and demand for this product seem to have been good,

---

[32] Vaudreuil to Minister, New Orleans, Dec. 6, 1744, *Ibid.*, C¹³A, 28:248-249.
[33] "A Chapter in Colonial History," *La. Hist. Quart.*, VI, 4, 663. For further information on this subject, see Vaudreuil to Minister, New Orleans, Aug. 25, 1743, *Arch. Nat., Col.*, C¹³A, 28:185; Minister to Vaudreuil and Salmon, Versailles, Jan. 13, 1744, *Ibid.*, B, 78:13.
[34] Vaudreuil and Le Normand to Minister, Jan. 4, 1745, *Ibid.*, C¹³A, 29:7ᵛ-8; Minister to Vaudreuil and Le Normand, Versailles, Oct. 9, 1747, *Ibid.*, B, 85:14ᵛ; same to same, Apr. 30, 1746, *Ibid.*, B, 83:20.
[35] Father Vivier to Father ————, June 8, 1750, Thwaites, *Jes. Rel.*, 69, 142-145. Wine was very little produced according to one authority. Memoir on Louisiana in 1740, *Arch. Nat., Col.*, C¹³C, 1:138. I have limited this discussion to agriculture in the upper country, and have not attempted to discuss farming in lower Louisiana.
[36] We often find mention of Illinois livestock in the western country. Sieur Charly, the farmer of the Miami post, was able to lend the government twenty-four horses in July, 1747, to help make the portage near that post on the occasion of a party of Indians being led to Detroit for conferences. See expense account drawn by Sieur Charly on July 3, 1747, totalling 2,007 livres, 10 sols, *Arch. Nat., Col.*, C¹¹A, 89:360ᵛ-361. These horses doubtless came from the Illinois. It is noticeable also that the expense accounts of the Miami post, the Wea post, and the post of River St. Joseph show more mention of purchases of beef and bacon than do those farther north. Here are the prices paid for livestock at these posts: oxen, 150 livres to 220 livres, cows, 200 livres, calves, 30 livres, large swine, 100 livres. For a description of how cattle and horses were raised in a semi-wild state on the "peninsula" called "La Pointe de Bois," see Father Vivier to Father ————, Nov. 17, 1750, in Thwaites, *Jes. Rel.*, 69, 217-222. The Memoir of 1746 gives the total of livestock in Louisiana as 10,000. *Arch. Nat., Col.*, C¹³A, 30:256 ff.

and the Illinois country was fast becoming the granary of Louisiana if not of all New France. As early as 1735, the king's troops in Martinique and San Domingo were supplied with Illinois flour.[37] By 1740, several posts of the western country, as well as New Orleans, were supplied partly or wholly with flour from this section.[38] In 1741 the descending convoy brought to New Orleans 125,000 lbs. of flour.[39] In 1742, however, continued heavy rains during the harvest did such great damage to the Illinois grain that there was hardly enough to feed the *habitants* and the garrison there.[40] For some reason, the crop of the following year seems to have been poor.[41]

The winter of 1744-1745 was very mild,[42] and the Illinois wheat crop seems to have been good, but there was difficulty in disposing of the crop. A large shipment of flour had come over from Rochefort that year on the king's ship. Then, too, a Dutch merchantman loaded with flour put into port at New Orleans, on excuse of seeking a mate, and the captain asked for permission to trade. This was finally refused, but it was said the Illinois men could hardly sell their flour.[43] In spite of the threatened revolt of the Illinois Indians in 1747, the harvest was said to have been good. In 1749 the minister, while considering the return of the Illinois country to the Canadian government, was careful to safeguard the export of Illinois flour to the southward, and encouraged an increase in its production by the promise that some "preference in the sale of this flour at New Orleans" should be considered.[44] All in all, the grain crop in the Illinois was important enough to play a large part in the economic and political life of New France, and especially of Louisiana.

The Canadian government was very anxious to increase the agricultural growth and development of the country. In 1743 an ordinance was

---

[37]In that year 3,000 *quintals*, or hundredweights, were bargained for at 13 livres, 10 sols, per cwt., including the barrels and cost of delivery to the said posts. Minister to Diron D'Artaguette, Versailles, Sept. 20, 1734, *Arch. Nat., Col.*, B, 62:81-82ᵛ. Flour rose constantly in price throughout the decade at the posts of the western country. In 1740, according to expense accounts, it averaged 20 livres per cwt. at Michilimakinac. In that same year, it brought 50 livres at the Miami, this due to scarcity. By 1745 it had dropped to 18 livres there, but in 1747 it was back to 30 livres. Corn ranged from 10 livres to 30 livres per *minot*. As was the case with livestock, flour seems to have been more plentiful at the Wea post, at River St. Joseph, and at the Miami than at Detroit or Michilimakinac. At least, it was issued more often. The *minot* according to an editor's note in Kalm was equal to two English bushels. Thwaites estimated it at three, which is certainly too high. On the basis of 39 *litres* it would equal 1.072 bushels.
[38]Memoir on Louisiana, 1740, *Arch. Nat., Col.*, C¹³A, 26:192ᵛ. That year was one of abundant harvest. La Loere Flaucourt to Salmon, July 29, 1740, *Ibid.*, C¹³A, 26:192ᵛ.
[39]Bienville to Minister, Sept. 30, 1741, New Orleans, *Ibid.*, C¹³A, 26:97-106.
[40]Bienville to Minister, Feb. 4, 1743, New Orleans, *Ibid.*, C¹³A, 28:33ᵛ-34.
[41]Vaudreuil to Minister, New Orleans, May 10, 1744, *Ibid.*, C¹³A, 28:222-222ᵛ. Only a small amount of flour was said to have come down to New Orleans that year by the convoy. A small amount was sent to Mobile for use of the sick only. Vaudreuil to Loubois, Aug. 2, 1744, *Vaudreuil Mss.*, 53.
[42]Kalm, *op. cit.*, III, 247.
[43]Le Normand to Minister, New Orleans, Apr. 8, 1746, *Arch. Nat., Col.*, C¹³A, 30:144ᵛ-145. The shipment to New Orleans that year amounted to 100,000 lbs. Vaudreuil to Minister, Mobile, Apr. 12, 1746, *Ibid.*, C¹³A, 30:57.
[44]Minister to Vaudreuil, Fontainebleau, Nov. 4, 1748, *Ibid.*, B, 87:15-15ᵛ. Under date of June 22, 1748, we find record of a sale in New Orleans of 29,841 lbs. of Illinois flour "delivered this day," this evidently being a part of the 1747 harvest. Records of the Superior Council, *La. Hist. Quart.*, XIX, 4, 1099. The harvest in the Illinois in 1748 was very bad. D'Auberville to Minister, New Orleans, May 9, 1749, *Arch. Nat., Col.*, C¹³A, 33:115-116.

issued by the king reforming the system of land grants, and intrusting future grants to the governor and intendant.[45] This was followed in 1747 by an ordinance which was intended to increase the size of farms so as to encourage more extensive cultivation. It was provided that no landowner might build a house and homestead on any plot containing less than forty-five square *arpents* in area.[46] Four years later, another ordinance was issued forbidding country people from migrating to the towns without written permission—this to keep them on the land in the interest of agriculture. Public works (work on the Quebec fortifications especially) were enticing them to leave their farms.[47]

The king was especially interested in the development of a strong agricultural community at Detroit, this the better to control the Indians as well as to reduce expenses of administration by the production of food for the garrisons there and at other places near at hand. In 1742, orders were given to set up a "sedentary command" at that post, consisting of a permanent resident commandant, devoted to the encouragement of agriculture and settlement of the post in particular, a deputy of the intendant, an almoner, an interpreter, and a surgeon. The support of these officials as well as of the *corps de garde* at the post was to be based on the proceeds from the sale of *congés* for the fur trade at the post. An annual sum of 1,500 livres was also to be set aside for Indian presents. The transportation of supplies, clothing, and other goods necessary for the support of these officers and the garrison was to be charged as a burden to the *voyageurs* coming up each year for the trade.[48] M. Céloron was sent there to assume the new command in 1742, but soon asked to be recalled on account of bad health. In 1743 Baron Longeuil succeeded him, but the governor abolished the new system and reverted to the old, claiming that such an important post should remain as a reward to those officers who distinguished themselves in the military service.[49] Faced with the outbreak of war with the English, the minister agreed to this change, and the plans for the development of the Detroit settlement were laid aside until after the war.[50]

Though a few settlers went to Detroit in 1743 on the basis of the *gratis congés*, this number was necessarily small. In 1749 after the return

---

[45]*Edits, Ordonnances*, I, July 17, 1743, 572-574.
[46]*Ibid.*, Apr. 28, 1745, 585-586. This ordinance did not apply to town dwellers. Bigot in 1749 ordered the destruction of certain houses built in defiance of this ordinance. *Ibid.*, June 25, 1749, II, 200.
[47]*Ibid.*, II, Apr. 20, 1749, 399-400.
[48]Free trading *congés* were to be issued to settlers who would come there. They were then to remain permanently on land granted them. Memoir of the King to Beauharnois and Hocquart, Fontainebleau, Apr. 30, 1742, *Arch. Nat., Col.*, B, 74:503-511. See also Memoir of the King to Beauharnois and Hocquart. May 31, 1743?, *Ibid.*, B, 76:436ᵛ-437.
[49]Beauharnois to Minister, Sept. 17, 1743, Quebec, *Ibid.*, C¹¹A, 79:110ᵛ-111ᵛ. Pierre Joseph Céloron, Sieur de Blainville (1693-1759). Paul Joseph Le Moyne de Longueuil, fourth baron (1701-1778), was a brother to Bienville and Iberville.
[50]Memoir of the King to Beauharnois and Hocquart, Versailles, Mar. 24, 1744, *Ibid.*, B, 78:325ᵛ-326. The governor and intendant opposed the new system, claiming it would tend to encourage the commandant in idleness and sloth. Beauharnois and Hocquart to Minister, Quebec, Oct. 12, 1744, *Ibid.*, C¹¹A, 81:29ᵛ-30.

of peace, the king re-established the system as set up in 1742 in all its essential parts. The Sieur Céloron was again given the command at a salary of 3,000 livres per year, with an extra gratification of 1,200 livres. The rank of major was then made an incident to this command, as had already been done in the case of the Illinois post. The minor posts near Detroit were placed under the jurisdiction of this same officer.[51] As an encouragement to settlers, the government offered to those willing to come flour rations for two years, as well as free tools with which to clear the lands. The settlers were asked to settle in villages for their mutual protection.[52]

In the spring of 1749, the king's engineer, M. Léry, accompanied a group of settlers to Detroit. The party went along with the trading convoy and the new temporary commandant, M. de Sabrevois. Céloron, who was then on his Ohio expedition, was to go up as soon as he returned. At Montreal they received seeds of fruits and grains of various kinds, as well as some grape vines which had been prepared there.[53] Forty-six settlers had already been sent there the year before, all said to have been from the Montreal district. Five thousand livres were also granted by Bigot to Father La Richardie to complete the rebuilding of his mission which had been destroyed in the Indian rebellion of 1747.[54]

From the beginning this new settlement was beset with troubles. In the first place, the colonists refused to obey the ordinance requiring them to settle in villages located close together, and instead went out wherever they pleased, seeking the best soils.[55] Father Bonnécamps reports that when he stopped there in 1749 on the return from the Ohio with Céloron's party, he found most of these settlers had "contented themselves with eating the rations that the king provided." Others he said had left the place, probably to follow the fur trade.[56] Some difficulty existed concerning the titles to the lands about Detroit which were still claimed by Cadillac's heirs,[57] but the poor quality of the settlers sent would seem to have accounted for the meager results of this attempt to increase the population there.

The account book of the Jesuit mission at Detroit in 1740-1741 shows

---

[51]Minister to La Jonquière and Bigot, Marly, May 14, 1749, *Ibid.*, B, 89:76-76ᵛ. The object of the king was chiefly to control the savages and to prevent in the future outbreaks such as that of 1747. The establishment of a strong French settlement at Detroit was thought to be the surest way to do this. It was not intended to extend the scheme to Michilimakinac on account of the poor soil there. Minister to La Jonquière, Versailles, May 19, 1750, *Ibid.*, B, 91:36-36ᵛ.

[52]Minister to Bigot, Apr. 30, 1750, *Can. Arch. Rep.*, 1905, I, 133.

[53]Journal of M. de Léry, May 26-June 6, 1749, in *Queb. Arch. Rep.*, 1926-27, 334 ff. Chaussegros de Léry was a famous engineer, who built the fortifications at Quebec. The Sabrevois brothers are confusing. They were Clement Sabrevois de Bleury (1702-81), and Christophe Sabrevois Sermonville (1701-?).

[54]La Jonquière and Bigot to Minister, Quebec, Oct. 5, 1749, *Wisc. Hist. Coll.*, XVIII, 30-32.

[55]*Ibid.*

[56]Bonnécamp's Journal, Thwaites, *Jes. Rel.*, 69, 189-193. Father Bonnécamps was professor of hydrography at the Jesuit college at Quebec.

[57]*Mich. Pion. and Hist. Coll.*, 34, 213-214. This also illustrates how difficult it was to colonize under a paternalistic system. The English colonies thrived because personal initiative was predominant. Quite the reverse was true in Canada where the government regulated everything closely.

that cleared land sold there at 20 livres per *arpent*, which incidentally was the cost of clearing the land. The Jesuits paid for both land and labor by barter of farm products.[58] Land was leased there in the year 1743 by the Jesuits, seed and farming implements as well as work animals being furnished. The crop was shared in halves, excepting Indian corn, all of which the tenant kept. In return, the tenant did carting and plowing for the Jesuits, and he could use their animals for his own carting. His wife also did the laundry for the mission.[59]

According to Kalm, the system of allowing a third of the land to lie fallow was used farther east, and this was probably necessary at Detroit,[60] especially after fields had been cultivated for some years. The yields must have been poor, judging from the Jesuits' account book for the year 1750.[61] Still, the high prices prevailing must have made agriculture at Detroit profitable for those interested in it. It is safe to assume that the purchases of the government at the posts during this decade were adequate to keep the demand lively.

The prices of grain varied greatly according to the demand of the post for it. Thus in 1740, Indian corn was bought at 15 livres per *minot* at Detroit by the government, it probably being more dear in the private trade.[62] In 1744, however, it brought only 7 livres per *minot* according to Detroit expense accounts. The war and the Indian rebellion a few years later caused it to soar again. At Michilimakinac, there was a poor harvest in 1741 and 1742 which caused very high prices—much above those of 1740. Thus corn in 1740 sold at 13 livres per sack there, and in 1741-1742 at 20 to 25 livres per sack. By 1743 it was back to 15 livres and fell to about 11 livres even during the early years of the war. During 1747 when the Indian revolt occurred it rose to 20 livres again. Prices at the more distant posts, such as the Wea, the Miami, and *La Baye* were always higher due to transportation expense. In any case, prices at the western posts were at least two times as high as at Quebec.[63]

It is doubtful if livestock were kept at Michilimakinac. There seem to have been a considerable number of cattle in the neighbourhood of Detroit,

---

[58]Thwaites, *Jes. Rel.*, 69, 245-253.
[59]The following seed and equipment were issued to the tenant to be returned to the landlord at the end of the six years lease, all losses to be made good: 6½ *minots* wheat, a new plow complete with its wheels, a cart, with almost new wheels, a new sled, two Illinois oxen (bison?), one Illinois cow, two mares worth 80 livres each, and two cows and a yearling heifer bred at Detroit. This whole outlay was valued at 400 livres. Later three extra Illinois heifers were supplied to the tenant to replace three lost. Two of these had been killed by accident, one by falling off a cliff, a second by the dogs of an Indian, and the third had been requisitioned by the post commandant to feast some Indians. Thwaites, *Jes. Rel.*, 69, 253-257.
[60]Kalm, *op. cit.*, III, 157-158.
[61]Thirty-seven *minots* of wheat? (the word is blank in Ms.), six *minots* of oats, and three-fourths *minot* of peas were sown that year. The harvest showed one hundred and fifty *minots* of wheat, sixteen *minots* of oats, and two *minots* of peas. There were also forty *minots* of Indian corn, and 1,600 onions raised, as well as some garlic. Thwaites, *Jes. Rel.*, 70, 55.
[62]The Jesuit account book shows that 18 livres per *minot* were received. *Ibid.*, 69, 247. The price was high that year due to consumptions for the Chickasaw campaign.
[63]The following prices for grain are quoted at Quebec in 1742: wheat or corn, 3 livres, 10 sols, to 4 livres per *minot*; peas, 4 livres to 4 livres, 10 sols, per *minot*; flour, 14 livres per quintal (cwt.). Hocquart to Minister, Quebec, June 11, 1742, *Arch. Nat., Col.*, C¹¹A, 77:277-283. Kalm gave the following as prices of grain at Montreal in September, 1749: wheat or corn, per *minot*, 3 livres (1 *écu*); peas, same as wheat; oats, per *minot*, 15-20 sols, "lately," 26-30 sols. *Op. cit.*, III, 299-301.

if one can judge by reference to them in the expense accounts.[64] On the other hand, cattle are not mentioned at Michilimakinac in the expense bills, while there is no reference to hogs at either post.[65] Bacon, though sometimes mentioned in the expense accounts, is uncommon, especially at Detroit and Michilimakinac.[66] In 1750 we find mention of the sending of an ass from France for breeding purposes.[67]

Sheep are not mentioned in the documents of this time concerning the western country, though they were quite common in the St. Lawrence country according to Kalm. Experiments to determine the quality and suitability of the wool from the neck of the bison were conducted in France with the view of using this product for French manufactures. Samples of this wool were requested both from Canada and from Louisiana by the minister, at the instance of the comptroller general of finances, M. Machault. It was thought that this wool would prove suitable for the manufacture of stockings and hats. M. Michel, *ordonnateur* of Louisiana, reported it unfit for the manufacture of stockings in any case, and he thought it could not be used in the hat manufactures unless some coarser fiber were added to it. The minister thought that the small amount of wool to be gotten from each beast would not justify its being killed for that purpose. It was also proposed that the dependability on the buffalo as a source of wool was not sure.[68] La Galissonière saw in the great hordes of bison an inexhaustible supply of meat and wool which would play an important part in the economy of the west in the future. In addition he thought the species could be domesticated as work animals if they were caught young and gelded. This was doubtless done to some

---

[64]See expense account, dated Oct. 17, 1747, for cattle furnished by Jacques Boucher at Longueuil's order. The number is not given, but the bill was scaled down by Hocquart from 316 livres to 136 livres. *Arch. Nat., Col.,* C¹¹A, 117:143-143ᵛ. On Oct. 22, 1747, Charles Courtois furnished Longueuil eight beeves, corn and other produce amounting to 3,871 livres, 16 sols. This was scaled down by Bigot to 3,710 livres, 16 sols. *Ibid.,* C¹¹A, 117:118. Dumont says cattle had been secured in the Illinois at 200 livres each for Bienville's Chickasaw campaign of 1739-1740, while horses cost 150 livres each. *Dumont Ms.,* 289. The number of cattle on the farm of the Jesuits mentioned indicates cattle were rather easy to get, either of French breed, or of Illinois stock (bison). There is evidence, however, that the French colonies imported beef and salted meats from foreign countries, though these products more than likely went to the sugar islands rather than to Canada or Louisiana. Thus the decree of August 27, 1738, supplementing a decree of June 18, 1737, allowed French ships to carry Irish beef, salt meat, salt salmon, butter, fats, and candles to the French colonies, this to be permitted for three years. *Recueuils de Règlemens, Edits, Declarations et Arrêts, Concernant le Commerce,* etc., 111-112. Similar decrees in 1740 and 1741 applied to the importation of salt meat from the Cape Verde Islands and Denmark. *Ibid.,* 113-116. Another decree in 1741 went so far as to allow the export of salt from France to the Cape Verde Islands free of export duty, the salt to be used in the meat industry. *Ibid.,* 116, 120.

[65]The only mention of livestock in the Michilimakinac bills is one instance dated June 15, 1747, in which one Lavoine Chevalier furnished a horse valued at 160 livres for an Indian feast. *Arch. Nat., Col.,* C¹¹A, 117:383.

[66]Hogs are mentioned as being bought only at the River St. Joseph post, according to the expense accounts studied. Hocquart allowed 100 livres for large hogs. May 13, 1746, *Ibid.,* C¹¹A, 117:459. Kalm gives the following as prices that were paid for farm animals at Montreal in September, 1749. These prices are supplied by M. De Couange, Montreal merchant: horse, "middling" quality, 40 livres, good, 100 livres; cow, 50 livres; sheep, 5-6 livres; hog, (one year old, 150 lbs.), 15 livres. The merchant told Kalm that this was a fair-sized hog, but that he had heard of one among the Indians which weighed 400 lbs.

[67]Minister to Bigot, Feb. 3, 1750, *Can. Arch. Rep.,* 1905, 1, 130.

[68]Controller General to La Galissonière, Versailles, Mar. 24, 1748, *Arch. Nat., Col.,* C¹¹A, 92:368-368ᵛ; Minister to Hocquart, Apr. 1, 1748, *Can. Arch. Rep.,* 1905, 1, 108; Minister to the Controller General, Versailles, Apr. 1, 1748, *Arch. Nat., Col.,* B, 88:41ᵛ; Apr. 17, 1748, *Ibid.,* B, 88:51; Minister to M. Michel, Dec. 16, 1748, *Ibid.,* B, 87:32ᵛ; Minister to Bigot, Versailles, Apr. 11, 1749, *Ibid.,* B, 89:10-10ᵛ; Michel to Minister, Aug. 6, 1749, *Ibid.,* C¹³A, 34:108-109.

POPULATION AND INDUSTRY   47

extent, as the above accounts of the "Illinois cattle" at Detroit seem to indicate.[69] In their wild state, he thought they could be of great use if rounded up in parks for slaughter, the meat to be salted down and exported in competition with Irish beef.[70]

Besides agriculture and the fur trade, the only industry of any significance in the western country was mining, which consisted chiefly of lead mining in the Illinois country. The mining industry in the Illinois had been put in the hands of the Sieur Renault and his associates under the Company of the Indies. In 1740 Renault surrendered his concession, finding himself in debt to the amount of 158,665 livres. His rights reverted to the king, and two other persons were then sent to work the mines. According to the report of 1741, the mine then worked was located on the Missouri side some fifteen leagues from Kaskaskia, which would place it near the Meramec River. At this time also the Galena deposits were being investigated. Enough lead was produced to supply the needs of the posts of the western country as well as to export some to New Orleans and even to France. When this mine was worked to capacity it was said to have yielded 40,000 lbs. annually.[71]

Though the minister asked repeatedly for detailed reports upon the working of the lead mines, none seem to have been made during the decade.[72] Nevertheless, lead was being produced in considerable quantities. In 1743, M. Salmon allowed 30,000 lbs. of Illinois lead to be shipped to France as ballast on the king's ship.[73] De Bertet, who assumed the Illinois command in 1743, took a great interest in the mines, especially in prospecting. He sent to France in 1744 several samples of lead ore taken from different places, and also some copper ore which he had procured from the Indians. This officer requested that some convicted salt smugglers be sent to the Illinois to work in the mines for three years, after which they would be given their freedom.[74]

The minister continually emphasized the promotion of agriculture instead of mining, considering that a strong and stable colony was necessary before the mines could be adequately worked. He did, however,

---

[69] See *supra*, p. 45, note 59.
[70] Memoir on the French Colonies of North America, 1750, *Doc. Rel. to the Col. Hist. of N. Y.*, X, 230-231.
[71] Bienville and Salmon to Minister, New Orleans, Apr. 25, 1741, *Arch. Nat., Col.*, C¹³A, 26:11-12. Minister to Bienville and Salmon, Versailles, Mar. 19, 1740, *Ibid.*, B, 70:448-448ᵛ. Alvord in the book, *The Illinois Country*, 209, leaves the impression that Renault surrendered his concession in 1744.
[72] Minister to Vaudreuil and Salmon, Versailles, Oct. 22, 1742, *Arch. Nat., Col.*, B, 74:662-662ᵛ. See also Minister to Vaudreuil, Versailles, Jan. 1, 1744, *Ibid.*, B, 78:6; Vaudreuil and Le Normand to the Minister, Jan. 4, 1745, *Ibid.*, C¹³A, 29:5ᵛ-6ᵛ. The latter indicates such a report was being prepared in the Illinois.
[73] Salmon to Minister, New Orleans, July 20, 1743, *Ibid.*, C¹³A, 28:105-105ᵛ. The minister granted permission to continue to send lead this way when there was room for it. Minister to Salmon, Versailles, Jan. 13, 1744, *Ibid.*, B, 78:16. Hocquart in 1743 estimated the total lead production of the Illinois at 75,000 lbs. Hocquart to Minister, Nov. 2, 1743, *Ibid.*, C¹¹A, 80:270.
[74] Vaudreuil to Minister, New Orleans, Dec. 6, 1744, *Ibid.*, C¹³A, 28:249-250ᵛ. Vaudreuil to Minister, New Orleans, Oct. 30, 1745, *Ibid.*, C¹³A, 29:91ᵛ-92. The samples of copper ore sent proved so poor that they were said not to be worth working. Minister to Vaudreuil and Le Normand, Apr. 30, 1746, *Ibid.*, B, 83:312.

promise to send over a dozen *faux sauniers* for the mines.[75] The war with the English upset the plans for sending over the *faux sauniers,* and little seems to have been done toward further development of the mines until peace returned.[76]

In 1747 a Portuguese mining engineer secured permission to prospect in the Miami River region and other places for copper. After some delay, he went out in 1748, but seems to have done nothing.[77] In 1750 he was prospecting, along with a Spaniard, and gave a very favorable report upon the possibilities of the mines, especially of those producing lead.[78] Salt was produced near Kaskaskia in quantities sufficient for the use of the Illinois[79] and the neighboring posts, including those of Canada.[80]

The copper deposits about Lake Superior had long been known to the French. In 1734, Sieur Denys La Ronde went out to command the post at Chequamigon, and began to prospect for copper. Returning to Montreal in 1736, he engaged two German miners in the following year,[81] who were, however, delayed at Montreal until the spring of 1738. La Ronde followed them, and with much difficulty got them to do some prospecting in company with his son. He himself remained at Chequamigon to pacify the Sauteur who had lately taken up arms against the Sioux of the Lakes. The younger La Ronde with six white men, including the two miners, set out for the discoveries. Ascending the River Sainte Anne, they found two mines, one on the left and one on the right bank of the river. These the German miners pronounced as good as the best in their own country according to La Ronde's report. Six leagues farther to the west, on Black River, they found a third mine which promised much. In 1739, after a fourth site had been located, La Ronde led the two Germans back to Quebec, leaving his son to build a fort and a forge on the River Sainte Anne. He was also to build a forty-ton boat for

---

[75]Minister to Vaudreuil, Jan. 1, 1744, *Ibid.,* B, 78:441ᵛ-442; Minister to Vaudreuil and Le Normand, Apr. 30, 1746, *Ibid.,* B, 83:312-313; Minister to Vaudreuil, Versailles, Apr. 25, 1746, *Ibid.,* B, 83:10. Direct orders were given in 1746 to De Bertet to leave the exploitation of mines for the present, and encourage agriculture. "Although the exploitation of the mines which are found in the Illinois region cannot fail to be of interest, there must not at present be any consideration of undertaking it. There is another object which deserves preference to all else; and this is the culture of the land." Minister to De Bertet, Paris, May 19, 1746, *Ibid.,* B, 83:321. Even the *faux sauniers* to be sent were recommended more for agriculture than for the mines. Minister to Vaudreuil, Versailles, Jan. 1, 1744, *Ibid.,* B, 78:7.
[76]Minister to Vaudreuil, Versailles, Apr. 25, 1746, *Ibid.,* B, 83:10. Some were promised at the end of the war. An instance is given at this time in which a salt smuggler's wife and children were sent at government expense to join him in Louisiana. Minister to Vaudreuil and Le Normand, Versailles, *Ibid.,* B, 83:20ᵛ. Of course, lead was mined all the while. In 1745 we find a record of 522 bars being sent to France from New Orleans. Surrey, *The Commerce of Louisiana,* 204. The price of lead remained during this decade almost without variation at 20 sols per pound according to the expense bills of the posts. This shows that the supply was always adequate for the demand, even in emergencies.
[77]Minister to Vaudreuil, Versailles, Oct. 9, 1747, *Arch. Nat., Col.,* B, 85:16; Vaudreuil to Minister, May 24, 1748, *Ibid.,* C¹³A, 32:65.
[78]Father Vivier to Father ———, at the Illinois, Nov. 17, 1750, Thwaites, *Jes. Rel.,* 69, 221-223.
[79]"A Chapter in Colonial History," *La. Hist. Quart.,* VI, 4, 564-565.
[80]Father Vivier to Father ———, at the Illinois, Nov. 17, 1750, Thwaites, *Jes. Rel.,* 69, 221-223.
[81]See *Arch. Nat., Col.,* C¹¹E, 13:251ᵛ, which is a record of La Ronde's life. He died in 1741, but his son who bore his name continued his work.

POPULATION AND INDUSTRY 49

use in moving materials to and from Sault Sainte Marie. Twelve carpenters were sent to assist him, and by 1740 it was reported that these works had been finished. It was La Ronde's intention to import French miners to work the mines, but in this he was opposed by the governor and intendant.[82]

In spite of the favorable report of the copper deposits as discovered by La Ronde's expedition in 1738 and 1739, the samples sent to France did not assay satisfactorily, and La Ronde died suddenly in 1741, leaving his son deeply in debt.[83] La Ronde the younger held the post for some years after his father's decease, exploiting the fur trade in that region, and paying off the debts of his father.[84]

Such was the actual state of the great western country, its people, and their industry in the 1740's. In passing it would be interesting to notice what the French thought would be the future of these vast regions. La Galissonière in 1750 summed the matter up as follows: "The question is not whether Colonies shall in future be established or not; they are established, and most of them firmly established. It is to be determined whether they will be handed over to jealous neighbors, whose entire ambition is to strip France of them."[85] This was doubtless the question in the minds of most Frenchmen at that time. But if the colonies were to remain in French control, what would be their future? To this question, La Galissonière also gave a reply, saying, "We must not flatter ourselves that our Continental Colonies; that is to say, this (Canada) and Louisiana, can ever compete in wealth with the adjoining English Colonies, nor even carry on any very lucrative trade; . . . ." The fur trade he saw as one whose profits were yearly diminishing, and the difficulties of navigation in the vast interior he thought would keep other profitable trade away.[86] Peter Kalm, on the other hand, saw in her colonies "the foundation to the rise of France," and lamented that his own country (Sweden) had allowed her hold on her American possessions to lapse.[87]

As far as the western country was concerned, La Galissonière envisioned it as the future home of a large French population, which would in time offset on the land the advantage England possessed over France on

---
[82]Beauharnois and Hocquart to Minister, Jan. 28, 1738, *Ibid.*, C¹¹A, 70: 253-254; Memoir of La Ronde on the copper mines of Lake Superior, Oct. 12, 1740, *Ibid.*, C¹¹E, 13:255-256.
[83]Memoir on the mines by Beauharnois and Hocquart, Jan., 1741, *Ibid.*, C¹¹A, 76:302-302ᵛ; Beauharnois to Minister, Quebec, May 12, 1741, *Ibid.*, C¹¹A, 16:237-239ᵛ. La Ronde died of apoplexy on Mar. 24, 1741. The minister reported "great difficulties" in the exploitation of the mines there. Minister to M. Grassin, Marly, Feb. 17, 1740, *Ibid.*, B, 71:51-51ᵛ; same to M. Saur, *Ibid.*, 51. Memoir of the King to Beauharnois and Hocquart, Marly, May 13, 1740, *Ibid.*, B, 70:359-363ᵛ. La Ronde had been financed by Sieur Charly at Montreal.
[84]Memoir of the King to Beauharnois and Hocquart, Marly, May 12, 1741, *Ibid.*, B, 72:382-386ᵛ.
[85]Memoir on the French Colonies in North America, 1750?, *Doc. Rel. to the Col. Hist. of N. Y.*, X, 221.
[86]La Galissonière to Minister, Quebec, Sept. 1, 1748, *Ibid.*, X, 134.
[87]Kalm, *op. cit.*, III, 110.

the sea. He especially advocated the development of the Illinois country as a part of this scheme.[88] In response to this, preparations were made to send additional settlers to the Illinois from France in 1750.[89] La Galissonière was also interested in the development and future of Detroit. It was he who laid out the plans for the sedentary command established there in 1749.[90] He thought, in fact, that Detroit was better located and had a better soil than the Illinois. It was his contention that an agricultural population of a thousand people there would be enough to give the French the key to the control of the upper lakes region as well as of the Ohio and the Illinois.[91]

What was to be the future relationship of Canada and Louisiana to each other in the French colonial scheme? The answer to this question was vital to the destiny of the great western country. "The conservation of Canada and Louisiana are closely bound together, the possession of one of these would put the English in position to win over all the savages of that part of the continent, and to engage them either by persuasion or by force to assist them in their enterprises .... The increase of their riches would soon render them the arbiters of all Europe, where they have already too much influence."[92] La Galissonière considered Louisiana as the smaller sister of Canada, it being the role of the latter to protect and nourish the former. The settlement of the Illinois was to be accomplished by immigration from Canada, and the Illinois in turn would supply the people necessary to develop the whole of Louisiana.[93]

---

[88] La Galissonière to Minister, Quebec, Sept. 1, 1748, *Doc. Rel. to the Col. Hist. of N. Y.*, X, 135. A stable population in the Illinois he said would also serve to subjugate all the savage nations of that country, so that such revolts as that of 1747 could not happen. He saw the Illinois country as holding a key position both in respect to checking the English advance and in respect to the control of the Indians. He proposed sending married men there as soldiers and discharging them after a short term of service. Then, too, he thought thirty to forty salt smugglers should be sent there each year, and ten or twelve Canadian families. This increase of population and agriculture would shortly give New France a bulwark in the west.
[89] Vaudreuil to Minister, Sept. 24, 1740, *Arch. Nat., Col.*, C^{13}A, 34:277-277^v. These were evidently the salt smugglers which had been promised since 1744. Minister to Vaudreuil, Versailles, Sept. 26, 1750, *Ibid.*, B, 91:14.
[90] La Galissonière to Minister, Sept. 25, 1748, *Wisc. Hist. Coll.*, XVII, 499-501.
[91] Memoir on the French Colonies in North America, 1750?, *Doc. Rel. to the Col. Hist. of N. Y.*, X, 230.
[92] Memoir on Louisiana in 1746, *Arch. Nat., Col.*, C^{13}A, 30:280-281.
[93] Memoir on the French Colonies of North America, 1750?, *Doc. Rel. to the Col. Hist. of N. Y.*, X, 231-232. He also saw Canada as the future granary of the tropical regions.

Chapter III

THE FUR TRADE

The Company of the Indies held the monopoly of the beaver trade in America. Though this monopoly had once included the trade in other furs as well, the company, finding only the beaver trade profitable, had relinquished its control of the others entirely. The following discussion will be chiefly concerned with the trade in beaver, information on the trade in other furs being scarce.

In knowledge of the fur trade the French are said to have excelled the English. "They know all that affair better than we do Their Ministers are well inform'd which I doubt ours are not They take much pains to be inform'd & never fail to incourage such as can give information or any way improve their Trade & Interest & they constantly employ men of sufficient abilities for that purpose while we take no pains & know little else besides what we learn from their books." These are the words of Cadwallader Colden, a shrewd English observer of conditions of trade and Indian relations.[1] This view was shared by both Conrad Weiser and Sir William Johnson who admired French skill in trade with the savages as well as in diplomacy.[2] The secret of the French ability to maintain their commercial and diplomatic ascendancy over the savages in the face of great odds is partly to be explained in their systematic way of handling the trade. They believed in strict regulation in keeping with the best mercantilist theory of the day, a policy which worked well considering the other handicaps of the trade. The fact that they eventually lost to the English in the contest for the control of the trade was due to weaknesses of the French industrial system and to the greater distances over which French traders operated in carrying on the trade. They did not tolerate freedom of trade and open competition, seeing in these the ruination of prices as well as opportunities for corruption.[3] The control of the trade was in the hands of the government, private individuals being forbidden to trade except under license.[4]

---

[1] Colden to Peter Collinson, December ?, 1743, *The Colden Papers, N. Y. Hist. Soc. Coll.*, 1919, III, 42-44. The best account of the Canadian fur trade in this period is found in Innis, H. A., *The Fur Trade in Canada, An Introduction to Canadian Economic History*, New Haven, 1930. See also Burpee, L. J., "Highways of Fur Trade," *Trans. Roy. Soc. of Canada*, third ser., VIII, 183-192. Surrey, N. M. (Mrs.), *The Commerce of Louisiana During the French Regime, 1699-1763*, New York, 1916, is the best general account of Louisiana trade and commerce. The beaver trade in Louisiana was not large, especially since Canadian traders took most of the catch in the northern regions of that province. Though present throughout most of Louisiana, the beaver did not produce good fur in the south. Deerskins were the leading item in the Louisiana trade.

[2] Weiser to Peters, 1745, *Penn. Arch.*, first ser., I, 671.

[3] Vaudreuil to Minister, New Orleans, Aug. 25, 1743, *Arch. Nat., Col.*, C¹³A, 28:82-83. The governor here shows how lack of regulation of the trade had caused bad conditions to arise in the Illinois.

[4] Minister to Father Lavaud, Apr. 27, 1742, *Can. Arch. Rep.*, 1905, 1, 4. Here the missionaries are especially forbidden to trade.

The post trade was carried on at various times under three systems of exploitation—the system of farming, the license system, and the system of exploitation by the commandant of the post. In the farming system, the monopoly of the trade at a given post was granted, usually at public auction,[5] to some individual or company. Such a lease was usually granted for a term of three years at a definite price. The farmer agreed to exploit the post himself, or to send *engagés* to do it for him. He was restricted to a certain territory or to trading with certain tribes in the neighborhood of the post, and could send as many canoes with goods as he deemed necessary. The content of his cargoes was strictly regulated, especially as to the amount of liquor carried. The farmer was assured that the officer at the post would protect him in his trade monopoly, and do him justice, while the farmer, in his turn, would supply the commandant with fuel, lodging, and the conveyance of his supplies from Montreal. In case of extraordinary expenditures, the commandant was obliged to buy the goods from the farmer at cost in Montreal plus a certain percentage for transportation charges. The farmer usually provided the interpreter for the post, and he was allowed to maintain a smith for his own profit. Finally, he bound himself to pay the price of the lease yearly subject to the penalty of imprisonment for debt.[6]

Under the license system, private traders bought *congés* permitting them to trade at certain posts. Each *congé* designated the number of canoes the trader was allowed to send, the *engagés* who were to accompany him, as well as the route to be taken. In order to prevent un-

---

[5]This was limited. The government reserved the right to pass upon the "general qualifications" of bidders.
[6]For sample conditions under which a farmer held a post, see contract of Sieur St. Ange Charly, Montreal merchant, for the exploitation of the post of the Miamis in 1724. (*O. L. Schmidt Collection*, II, 326-327). In this contract the farmer paid 3,000 livres per year for the permit to trade, his contract lasting for three years. His field was limited to certain well established regions about the post, but he could send as many canoes as he deemed necessary. He agreed to take only a minimum number of men to the post in time of war (this in order not to weaken the defense of the colony), and of course he was required to secure the usual licenses for the canoes. Only four pots of liquor per man per canoe could be taken up to the post, though fifteen barrels (16 pots each) might be taken up yearly for the consumption of the post garrison, and the general trade. The former lessee was to cease trading as soon as the new one arrived, taking his goods to Detroit for disposal, though he might leave an agent at the Miamis to collect his debts. The officer at the post was forbidden to trade; on the other hand, he was required to protect the farmer against *coureurs de bois*, whose goods if found were to be forfeited to the farmer. The farmer on his part was bound to bring up to the post yearly, and at his own expense, 1,500 lbs. of goods for the commandant, including his trunk. In case of extraordinary expenditures, the commandant was to buy goods from the farmer at cost plus thirty per cent. The farmer maintained an interpreter at the post both for his own use and for that of the commandant. If any forges were established, they were to operate to the profit of the farmer. See also contract for exploitation of the post at La Baye in 1747. *Wisc. Hist. Coll.*, XVII, 451-455. The provision regarding liquor in this case was the same except that thirty or forty casks of liquor might be brought up for the general trade. Of course the farmer might sublet his post to others. In this case, the new lessees were subjected to all the terms of the farmer's contract, and in addition they agreed to certain other provisions especially regarding furnishings. (They usually agreed to buy these from the farmer if he were a merchant, as he commonly was.) The farmer was to receive the furs, taking pay for furnishings made and paying for the surplus at the Quebec price. The sub-lessees also were bound to submit their expenses to a yearly audit at the hands of the farmer, and they were singly and collectively responsible for the advances made by the farmer as well as for the rental of the post. Lastly, the farmer became the legal representative of the sub-lessees "to look after the interest of the partnership." See contract between Srs. Clignancourt, *et al.*, and Srs. Monière and Lechelle concerning the farm of *La Baye*, April 4, 1747, *O. L. Schmidt Coll.*, II, 250-251. A farmer or trader in his necessity might also voluntarily take in a partner; La Vérendrye once made Sieur Gamelin such a proposition on Gamelin's own terms. *Ibid.*, 373.

licensed individuals from going out with the canoes the role of each *engagé* was fixed. Holders of *congés* were also bound to carry in each canoe going out to the post a certain amount of goods for the king, such as supplies for the commandant, missionary, or interpreter. *Congés* were not sold at auction, but were issued upon application. Sometimes they were given *gratis* for certain reasons. The *engagé* was placed under contract with the *voyageur* who held the *congé*. He agreed to make the trip and return for a certain sum to be paid in peltries at the market price on his return to Montreal.[7] In the system of exploitation of the posts by the military commandant, this officer held a monopoly of the trade just as the farmer under the farming system.

The decade under consideration saw all three systems of exploitation of the post in use. For some years, the officers had been allowed to trade at their posts, but in 1742 the king ordered this system to be abolished and the farming system established. This change of policy was doubtless due to pressure from wealthy traders at Montreal and Quebec, though the excuse offered was that the "good of the service had been imperilled by the attention the officers had been giving to the trade."[8] Beginning in 1743, all posts, except Michilimakinac, Detroit, Chequamigon, and the posts of *La Mer d'Ouest,* were to be let out to farms at auction. Detroit and Michilimakinac were to be left on the *congé* footing, while Chequamigon and La Vérendrye's posts were to be left to the exploitation of the officers in command.[9] Officers in command of those posts farmed out or licensed to traders were to be paid a percentage of the proceeds of the post, except at Detroit. Here the system of a "sedentary command" was to be established as a part of the scheme to encourage settlement of the post and the development of agriculture.[10]

Beauharnois strongly objected to this change of policy. He claimed the Indians would be driven to trade with the English because of the fear that monopoly would mean higher prices.[11] He also pointed out that he had already made certain promises under the old system, and he objected

---

[7]Two hundred livres seems to have been the standard price for a trip from Montreal to Michilimakinac in 1730. See facsimile of an *engagement* in *Quebec Arch. Rep., 1930-31,* 385. In 1750, in the case of two canoes going up to La Vérendrye's posts for the government, the first was allowed 0,010 livres for wages for the crew of seven. The guide received 700 livres, the others from 320 to 450 livres each. The second, having a crew of six, was allowed 2,280 livres for the same item, the individual wages ranging from 310 to 500 livres. *Arch. Nat., Col.,* C¹¹A, 96:327.

[8]Minister to Hocquart, Fontainebleau, Apr. 20, 1742, *Ibid.,* B, 74:478 ff.

[9]Memoir of the King to Beauharnois and Hocquart, Fontainebleau, Apr. 30, 1742, *Ibid.,* B, 74:503-511. The posts established by La Vérendrye were referred to as "the posts of the western sea."

[10]A permanent staff was to be set up there, consisting of the commandant, with a permanent tenure, a deputy of the intendant, an almoner, an interpreter, and a surgeon. The commandant was to receive 3,000 livres yearly, the others 500 livres or less; 1,500 livres yearly was to be allowed for Indian presents. Agriculture and settlement of the land were to be encouraged by *gratis congés* for trade to those who would agree to settle there.

[11]The governor argued in justification of the old system, that the military officers took only a certain share of the proceeds of the posts. For example, he says the Detroit officer took only 3,000 livres yearly from the *voyageurs* there, and so with the one at River St. Joseph. The amount a trader took depended on his wits!

particularly to allowing the missionaries at some of the posts to operate the forges against which the Indians had complained.[12]

As to the plan to make Detroit a sedentary establishment, Beauharnois agreed the more readily because he was desirous of disposing of De Noyan, commandant at that post. Serious objections were raised as to the method proposed for having supplies and provisions brought up to the post by the *voyageurs,* on the ground that not enough allowance had been made for these things.[13] The same objections were made as to the application of the scheme to Michilimakinac.[14]

The post at Chequamigon was to be left to the younger La Ronde for two years, and La Vérendrye was to be allowed to continue to exploit his posts for a similar period, though the minister was seriously considering having him removed.[15]

The minister in reply to these arguments pointed out that the new scheme would not result in higher prices for goods at the posts. The governor was assured that the farmers in bidding would be careful not to put their bid so high as to be forced to raise their prices to the savages in order to make a profit on the trade.[16] The appearance of monopoly was disguised by ordering the farmers to establish more than one store at their posts so as to give the impression that competition was present.[17] However, only four posts—*La Baye,* Michipicoton, the Wea, and Temiscamingue—were farmed out in 1743, and this drew an order from the king to farm out the others the following year.[18]

Beauharnois, however, was not reconciled to the new system; he took occasion to point out how badly things went at Niagara, where Sieur Chalet, the farmer in charge, had raised his prices so high that the Indians had carried their furs to Oswego to such an extent that receipts had dwindled by 600 packets of furs.[19] At *La Baye,* Sieur Lusignan, the com-

---

[12]Beauharnois to Minister, Quebec, Sept. 5, 1742, *Arch. Nat., Col.,* C¹¹A, 77:94-97; Beauharnois and Hocquart to Minister, Oct. 8, 1742, *Ibid.,* C¹¹A, 78:378-385. The main argument was that the change of policy would ruin the governor's reputation with the savages, since he had promised them to do otherwise. Concerning the plan to pay the officers a percentage of the proceeds of the trade, it was argued that the officer would not have any certainty of support. It was suggested that the farmers be required to pay the officer one-half of his gratification in advance, the whole not to exceed 3,000 livres. It had long been the custom to allow the missionary to operate the forge at the posts, in order to help him to support the mission. The missionary supplied the tools and steel, and the smith built a charcoal forge and also assisted in getting the fuel at times. It was further agreed that the smith was to do the work brought to him by the Indians, and also the Jesuit's work, for his house or church. All receipts by the smith were divided with the Jesuit equally. The smith might or might not lodge with the missionary. If he worked for himself, he had to use his own iron. At the end of the lease (usually six years) he returned all tools, etc. See Thwaites, *Jes. Rel.,* 69, 241-245; *Ibid.,* 33.
[13]Under this scheme, 1,200 lbs. of baggage had been allowed to the commandant, and 600 lbs. each for the interpreter, surgeon, and other officers at the post. This baggage was to be brought up in the trader's canoes each year. The governor and intendant estimated that the commandant could drink that much weight in wine alone during the year! Memoir of Beauharnois and Hocquart, Detroit, Sept. 24, 1742, *Arch. Nat., Col.,* C¹¹A, 78:393-396. Pierre Jacques Payan de Noyan, Sieur de Chavois, (1695-?) was a nephew of Longueuil and Iberville. For his quarrel with Beauharnois, see *infra,* pp. 66-68.
[14]Hocquart and Beauharnois, Memoir on the Posts, Oct. 8, 1742, *Ibid.,* C¹¹A, 78:378-385.
[15]Memoir of the King to Beauharnois and Hocquart, Fontainebleau, Apr. 30, 1742, *Ibid.,* B, 74:503-511.
[16]Minister to Beauharnois, Versailles, Apr. 30, 1743, *Ibid.,* B, 76:403.
[17]Beauharnois to Minister, Quebec, Sept. 22, 1743, *Ibid.,* C¹¹A, 79:144-145ᵛ.
[18]Memoir of the King to Beauharnois and Hocquart, Versailles, Mar. 24, 1744, *Ibid.,* B, 78:326ᵛ.
[19]Beauharnois to Minister, Quebec, Oct. 9, 1744, *Wisc. Hist. Coll.,* XVII, 442-443.

mandant, came to open conflict with his farmer, Sieur Augé, over the exploitation of the trade. Lusignan charged Augé and others were trading openly with *coureurs de bois*. The traders, on their part, claimed that the commandant sought to prevent them from trading at all. Though Augé was recalled under ministerial approval, orders were given that the conduct of officers regarding their farmers should be kept under close observation. Céloron at Niagara was also named as an offender in this respect.[20]

The war with the English caused the question of trade regulation to be neglected, while it brought great confusion in the exploitation of the trade. At the end of the war, however, La Galissonière and Bigot took up the subject again and urged a return to the license system. The governor argued that competition between the traders at the posts would mean lower prices of goods for the savages. This, plus the normal return of lower prices incident to the restoration of peace, he hoped would be very attractive to the Indians. He said prices in Montreal were then 150 per cent of what they were before the war, and that traders could hardly keep from raising their prices at the posts accordingly. Bigot thought a part of this rise in prices was due to bargains made between the licensed traders or farmers and the commandants of the posts.[21]

The rising prices of goods, caused by the war and by competitive bidding of the farmers for the posts, is said to have been the cause of the beginning of the defection of the Indians of the upper country from the French. It was the governor's contention that the Indians at most posts were asking for the restoration of the license system, especially those about *La Baye* and River St. Joseph. He said the peace with the English would never cure the evils of the situation, though, of course, it would help. As a sort of palliative to the minister, La Galissonière recommended that the very distant posts such as Nepigon, Temiscamingue, Kamanistiquia, Michipicoton, and Chequamigon, where the Indians were so far away from English influence that they had not complained, might be left to the farmers, the others being returned to the license system.[22] The minister approved of the suggestion, stipulating that no officer should trade at any post, but should receive a fixed gratification according to rank. It was further ordered that the yearly payment of 10,000 livres for poor relief from the proceeds of the licenses should be continued.[23]

The problem of the *coureurs de bois* was always a serious one in regard to trade regulation. These men were illegal traders—men who disregarded the regulations of the government and carried on trade of their

---

[20]Minister to Beauharnois, Versailles, Apr. 28, 1745, *Arch. Nat., Col.*, B, 81:39ᵛ; Memoir of the King to Beauharnois and Hocquart, Versailles, Apr. 28, 1745, *Ibid.*, B, 81:289ᵛ-290. Paul Louis Dazenard, Sieur de Lusignan (1691-?) held many commands in the west, 1735-1746.
[21]Bigot to Minister, Oct. 22, 1748, *Wisc. Hist. Coll.*, XVII, 502.
[22]La Galissonière to Minister, Oct. 23, 1748, *Ibid.*, XVII, 503-504.
[23]Minister to La Jonquière and Bigot, Marly, May 4, 1749, *Ibid.*, XVIII, 25-27; La Jonquière and Bigot to Minister, Sept. 28, 1749, *Ibid.*, 29-30.

own. They received their supplies from licensed French traders or from the English in exchange for their furs. Sometimes Indians served as agents between the *coureurs de bois* and their furnishers. The government continually tried to control them, by issuing orders for their arrest, by regulating the licenses more closely, and finally by sending out traders to compete with them on their own ground. In 1739, Hocquart issued an *ordonnance* regulating the *rôles* of *engagés* to the end of keeping vagabonds or other unlicensed individuals from going up with the traders.[24] In 1741, an edict of the king provided that *congés* might be issued to a number of traders to go out beyond the posts and trade in the woods.[25] We have noticed above that Lusignan laid the trouble at *La Baye* to illicit trade between the farmer and the *coureurs de bois*. In this case it was charged that a deal involving 6,000 livres had been made between them, the farmer exchanging merchandise for beaver. This business was terminated when Sieur Augé was arrested and sent back to Montreal.[26] Of course the *coureurs de bois* did not return for their punishment.[27] The French government blamed these outlaws also for the slow rate of growth of the colony in population, since most of them took Indian wives and not only deprived the colony of their own numbers, but also of their natural increase.[28] During the years of the war, and especially in 1746 and 1747, when the supply of goods was practically cut off for the western trade, the *coureurs de bois* grew in numbers and in prosperity. They became so numerous that La Galissonière considered catching some and deporting them as examples. He also suggested that they might be licensed as privateers, such a life being well suited to their temperament.[29]

In no other place was the problem of lawless elements more acute than in the Illinois. Miscegenation between the whites and natives was reported to have been unusually common there, as a consequence of which the missionaries had allowed whites and natives to intermarry freely.[30] Desertion, as we have seen, was common among the Illinois troops, and the fact that the Illinois lay at the outskirts of both colonies, with the boundary between them unsettled, led to additional abuses. *Voyageurs* licensed in Canada often disregarded the Illinois authorities, and unlicensed traders found protection in the fact that they could usually rely upon assistance from the Canadians.

As early as 1743, Vaudreuil had written the minister, that in order to

---

[24]Ordonnance, No. 278, June 17, 1739, *Arch. Nat., Col.*, C11A, 71:114-115.
[25]Twenty-five canoes were equipped with three men each to go into "*la profondeur de bois.*" No person was to hold such a permit two years in succession. King's Edict upon the Fur Trade, undated, *Collection de Documents*, III, 193.
[26]Beauharnois to Minister, Quebec, Oct. 25, 1744, *Arch. Nat., Col.*, C11A, 81:196-197v.
[27]Minister to La Jonquière, Versailles, Mar. 6, 1747, *Ibid.*, B, 85:2-2v.
[28]*Ibid.*
[29]La Galissonière to Minister, Oct. 21, 1747, *Ibid.*, C11A, 87:254-254v. This resulted only in further orders to commandants of the posts to apprehend these outlaws. Lists drawn up by the governor were sent to each commandant. Journal of Occurrences, 1747-48, *Doc. Rel. to the Col. Hist. of N. Y.*, X, 162.
[30]Minister to the Abbé de Brizacier, Versailles, undated, *Arch. Nat., Col.*, B, 62:88.

stop the abuses of the *coureurs de bois* and the frequent desertion from the garrison, "It would be necessary to take special steps to make sure of those who go there to trade." The minister encouraged Beauharnois and Vaudreuil to work out some plan by which they could cooperate to cut down these irregularities.[31] The Canadian governor, jealous of the possession of the Illinois by Louisiana, was not in a mood to cooperate, especially if cooperation meant the defining of a boundary line between the two colonies. A bitter controversy thus arose between the two governments over the boundary question, and all attempts to settle the matter or to remedy the abuses in the Illinois trade came to naught.[32]

The fur trade was carried on by means of an exchange involving raw furs and merchandise. Though some trading was done each spring at Montreal when the savages came to meet the governor and to receive their presents, most of it was done at the posts of the upper country, to which places the traders had carried their goods by canoes. The trading convoy usually left Montreal in May, reaching Detroit sometime in July. The traders departed to their several posts, disposed of their goods to the savages and French hunters and trappers, and then returned home loaded with peltries. The return trip was scheduled to be made in time for the canoes to reach Montreal before bad weather began in November. In the case of the more distant posts, the canoes did not return until the following spring, it being necessary to winter there. The articles suitable for the trade were those used by the savages and by the French woodsmen in their primitive life of hunting, trapping, and warfare.[33] In general, the French were careful to stock articles that were suitable for the trade; sometimes, however, improper goods were sent, especially in stocks for the government's stores, which seem to have been used oftentimes as depositories for shop-worn goods of French merchants—goods utterly useless even for presents for the savages.[34]

The furs chiefly in demand were: skins of the beaver (dry or fat), bear, raccoon, otter, red fox, mink, fisher, wolf, and deer. Of these the

[31] Minister to Beauharnois, Apr. 28, 1745, *Wisc. Hist. Coll.*, XVIII, 5-6.
[32] In general, the Louisiana governor contended for complete control of the Illinois trade and insisted on extending the boundaries of Louisiana as far north as the Wisconsin River. The Canadian authorities were unwilling to give in and the Minister seemed inclined to favor them. At one time he proposed the return of the Illinois country to Canada. Lack of space does not permit giving an account of this interesting controversy which has been worked out in detail.
[33] The journey from Montreal to Michilimakinac and return consumed about five months, while two additional months were required to go from Michilimakinac to the Illinois. From Quebec the time required to go to Michilimakinac was half again greater than that from Montreal. See Massicotte, E.-Z., "Arrêts, Edits, Ordonnances .... dans la Palais de Justice de Montreal," *Trans. Roy. Soc. of Canada*, third ser., XI, 169, note. Pouchot gives the following as the most common articles which were sent up to the posts: hunting guns, lead, balls, powder, steel for striking fire, gun-flints, gun screws, knives, hatchets, kettles, beads, men's shirts, cloth (red and blue) for blankets and petticoats, vermillion and verdigris, tallow, blue and green ribbon of English weaving, needles, thread, awls, blue, white, and red rateen for making moccasins, woolen blankets of three points and a half, three, two, and one and a half of Léon cloth, mirrors framed in wood, hats trimmed fine, and in imitation, with variegated plumes or in red, yellow, blue and green, hoods for men and children of fringed rateen, galloons, real and imitation, brandy, tobacco, razors for the head, glass in beads made after the fashion of wampum, black wines, and paints. Pouchot, *op. cit.*, II, 49.
[34] See Pouchot, *op. cit.*, II, 47-48.

beaver was most desirable, though the French are said to have sought the skins of smaller animals in the Hudson Bay region. The smaller peltries were not sought to a great extent in Louisiana, chiefly because the milder climate of that region decreased the quality of the furs.[35] Deerskins and buffalo hides were more in demand. The Company of the Indies held the monopoly of the beaver trade; the trade in other furs was open to free exploitation. Since the trade in beaver so greatly exceeded that in other furs, and since there exists a general lack of information on the trade in other peltries, our discussion will be limited to the beaver trade.

In the latter 1730's, the French realized that they were losing trade to the English at Oswego, this being reflected in decreased receipts at Niagara and Frontenac. It was reported that the trade in peltries at these two posts decreased from 52,000 lbs. yearly to 25,000-35,000 lbs. between 1732 and 1736.[36] Beauharnois and Hocquart attributed this slump in trade to three causes: (1) the suppression of the brandy trade, (2) the bad quality of the *écarlatines*,[37] and (3) the low price of beaver.[38] The difference in the price paid by the French and the English was possibly the chief factor. In 1739, the English paid five shillings, five and one fourth pence per pound for prime beaver, while the French even after the increase in price in 1738 paid only 20 sols for summer or autumn beaver, and 55 sols for fat or dry skins of good quality. In addition there was a deduction of five per cent commission made on the French prices by the company.[39] After the increase in price in 1738 the French redoubled their efforts to enforce trade regulations, to the end of preventing trade with the English.[40] In regard to improving the quality of the *écarlatines*, little could be done. Undoubtedly the English cloths were of better quality, but mercantilist policies would not allow the French company to use them. Moreover, they could not depend on such a source in time of war.

A problem of equal difficulty was that of the liquor trade with the Indians. Both Hocquart and Beauharnois urged that the restrictions on the liquor trade be removed, especially at Niagara, where, it was argued, a plentiful supply of *eau de vie* would be adequate insurance against Indian canoes going to Oswego.[41] We have noticed in another chapter

---

[35] See Le Page Du Pratz, *Histoire de la Louisiane*, III, 377-378.
[36] Quoted in Innis, *op. cit.*, 89. Receipts of beaver by the company in 1737 were 124,000 lbs., whereas 180,000 lbs. had been expected. *Arch. Nat., Col.*, C¹¹A, 70:103-111.
[37] This is the current trade term for the red and blue cloths used by the savages for blankets and petticoats.
[38] Memoir to the King by Beauharnois and Hocquart, May 15, 1738, *Arch. Nat., Col.*, C¹¹A, 69:13-29ᵛ.
[39] Hocquart to the Directors of the Company of the Indies, Quebec, Oct. 16, 1738, *Ibid.*, C¹¹A, 70:103-111. See also Innis, *op. cit.*, 109.
[40] In 1737 Hocquart estimated the English harvest of beaver amounted to only 37,000 lbs. *Ibid.*
[41] Hocquart to Minister, Quebec, Oct. 26, 1740, *Arch. Nat., Col.*, C¹¹A, 74:306-309ᵛ. Beauharnois was of the opinion that the savages preferred the French *eau de vie* to the English rum, and said that 10,000-12,000 lbs. of extra beaver were collected at Quebec in 1739 by using liquor freely. Hocquart to the Company of the Indies, Quebec, Nov. 3, 1740, *Ibid.*, C¹¹A, 73:384-386.

that the church opposed the liquor traffic, and that the government had adopted a policy of regulation which would keep down the worst abuses without, however, stopping the trade.

The English were faced with the same problem. Sir William Johnson's success in his Indian policy at Mt. Johnson was owing not a little to his trade in rum, which more than once involved him in difficulties with his government.[42] In Pennsylvania, the governor reported that the laws regulating the rum trade could not be enforced, and disclosed that his government might be obliged to take the trade out of private hands as had already been done in New England.[43] Conrad Weiser says that the evil had so increased that the only remedy for it would have been to apply the death penalty to those who violated the laws in that respect.[44] In respect to the evil of the liquor trade, the English and the French were thus in agreement. Liquor, nevertheless, continued to be one of the major items of merchandise which the Indian received for his furs.

There were other abuses in the French trade besides the secret trade with the English at Oswego. We have seen something of how the *coureurs de bois* competed with licensed traders.[45] Detroit also bore a bad reputation in the matter of sending beaver to the English at Oswego through the medium of the savages. This business was shared by the licensed traders in many instances.[46] The governor and intendant were not over-zealous in enforcing the regulations of the trade for the absentee company, and there is reason to believe that they secretly allowed illicit trade to be carried on.[47] In any case, the receipts of beaver by the Company of the Indies, were yearly growing less, and in 1738, as we have seen, it had been necessary to raise the price. Attempts had also been made to increase the amount and quality of *écarlatines* sent for the trade.[48]

Any attempt to discuss the volume of the trade in the western country must necessarily meet with serious difficulties due for the most part to the inadequacy of materials. The large illegal trade can, of course, be studied only incidentally. The following table embodies in summarized form the available trade figures for the decade under consideration. It should be understood that these figures are far from complete. Then, too, figures for *congés* granted do not necessarily mean that the *congé*

---

[42]See Summons of the Indian Commissioners to Johnson, July 22, 1743, *Sir William Johnson Papers*, I, 19; Joseph Clement to Johnson, Old Condacktedie, Aug. 16, 1748, *Ibid.*, 180.
[43]Min. of the Council, July 31, 1744, *Penn. Col. Rec.*, IV, 740.
[44]See Weiser to ———, in Min. of the Council, Dec. 5, 1747, *Penn. Col. Rec.*, V, 167.
[45]Hocquart to the Directors of the Company of the Indies, Oct. 16, 1738, *Arch. Nat., Col.*, C¹¹A, 70:103-111.
[46]Hocquart to the Directors of the Company of the Indies, Nov. 3, 1740, *Ibid.*, C¹¹A, 74:384-386ᵛ.
[47]Bigot once admitted that he had allowed a secret trade in wool with New England. Messieurs Forant and Bigot to Minister, Louisbourg, Jan. 16, 1740, *Col. de Doc.*, III, 187.
[48]Memoir of the king to Beauharnois and Hocquart, Marly, May 13, 1740, *Arch. Nat., Col.*, B, 70:359-363ᵛ. The price of beaver as fixed in 1738 was 55 sols for fat and dry beaver of good quality, and 20 sols for all other grades. These prices are per pound of pelts. The term "fat" was applied to partly cured pelts, while "dry" pelts were those which had been completely cured. The difference between "fat" and "dry" is no longer noticed in the grading of furs, it being assumed that any pelt received is cured enough to prevent spoiling.

was actually used, since many things might happen to prevent a *voyageur* from completing his journey. The figures given include the trade in the Illinois country, but not in the rest of Louisiana.[49]

Year	Congés	Canoes	Men Engaged	Total Receipts (lbs.)
1740	32	57	336	147,000-148,000†
1741*	..	..	...	....
1742*	..	..	...	157,000
1743	54	68	417	200,000†
1744*	54	..	...	200,000†
1745	43	..	...	180,000†
1746	27	39	208	180,000†
1747	37	55	330	100,000-120,000†
1748	..	55	...	166,172
1749	..	72	434	....
1750	..	74	419	....

*The registers of *congés* for 1741, 1742, and 1744 are missing.
†Estimated receipts.

These figures, incomplete as they are, indicate a decided increase both in the number of canoes sent and in total receipts of beaver during the period 1740-1743. Except for the Chickasaw campaign of 1739-1740 and minor expeditions against the same enemy in the years immediately following, this was a period of peace. The engagement of northern Indians in this war might be expected to have taken some hunters away from the woods and so have reduced the total "catch" in those years. However, we must conclude that this factor was negligible.

Beginning with 1744 we have the outbreak of the war with the English, which shows its effect in the fall of receipts as indicated. This decline reaches the lowest point in 1747, which year saw the Indian rebellion in the Great Lakes region, with the result that trade was almost entirely cut off during the spring and summer months. Then, too, beginning in 1746 large numbers of western Indians went down to Montreal where they joined the French in the war against New England. The presence of the warriors at Montreal necessarily reduced the hunting of beavers in the upper country.

With the return of peace in 1748, our figures indicate a considerable increase in receipts, though the number of canoes engaged in the trade was no greater than in the previous year. In the two following years our figures show a great increase in the trade activity. Figures for receipts for the last two years of the decade unfortunately are missing, but from the number of canoes and men engaged, it can be assumed that the receipts would show considerable increases over those of the war period.

[49]These figures are compiled from various manuscript sources and from the registers of *congés* as published in the *Quebec Archives Reports*. Innis has also been consulted.

THE FUR TRADE 61

The period thus ends with evident increased activity on the part of the French in the western trade.

Another factor bearing on the volume of the trade was that of prices offered for beaver. Faced with declining receipts after 1745, due to increased trade difficulties, rising prices of merchandise, and scarcity of goods in Canada incident to the war, the French found it necessary to raise the price of beaver above the figures set in 1738. On the basis of an estimated increase of forty per cent in the price of merchandise, it was recommended that the price of dry winter beaver be raised to three livres, fifteen sols, per pound, and fat winter beaver to four livres per pound. The prices of dry summer beaver were to be put at twenty to thirty sols, depending on the quality.[50] These prices were approved and ordered to be put into effect in June, 1746.[51] Undoubtedly this increase in the price of beaver served to offset to a considerable extent the other disadvantages which the French met in the trade during the war period.

It was first stipulated that these new prices were to be in effect only for the duration of the war, but in 1747 the company agreed to continue to pay the war-time prices for one year after the restoration of peace, this undoubtedly having a heartening effect on the trade.[52] By 1748, however, the English price for first quality beaver was equal to four livres, twelve sols, in French money, or twelve sols above the French price. This difference is really greater than it at first appears when it is recalled that French prices were subject to a five per cent commission charge by the company, while English bills of exchange were also on a more favorable footing than the French. In spite of these facts, the company was anxious to lower the price, claiming a loss of over 100,000 livres in the period 1746-1747.[53] The price of beaver was actually reduced in 1749 and again in 1750.[54]

The effect of these price changes must of course be considered in relation to the prevailing price of merchandise at the posts. Though space does not permit the citing of figures, a study of the prices of goods as shown in the expense accounts at the western posts indicates there was a

[50]Beauharnois and Hocquart to Minister, Quebec, Oct. 15, 1744, *Arch. Nat., Col.*, C¹¹A, 81143 46ᵛ.
[51]Minister to Hocquart and Beauharnois, Mar. 17, 1745, *Can. Arch. Rep.*, 1905, I, 39; Beauharnois and Hocquart to Minister, Quebec, Sept. 18, 1746, *Arch. Nat., Col.*, C¹¹A, 85:7. This increase was calculated to put French prices on a par with prices then paid by the English. Compare with prices of beaver at Albany in March, 1745/46: fat beaver, five shillings; dry beaver, four shillings, six pence. *Sir William Johnson Papers*, I, 47-48.
[52]Minister to La Jonquière and Hocquart, Mar. 6, 1747, *Can. Arch. Rep.*, 1906, I, 84. One writer said in regard to this: "I shall observe that as long as the beavers are at a high price, the voyageurs redouble their industry to encourage the Indians to winter in beaver country . . . ." Quoted by Innis, *op. cit.*, 105.
[53]See Memoir on Beaver Trade, 1748, *Arch. Nat., Col.*, C¹¹A, 93:10-12ᵛ. The writer of this document attacks the company violently and suggests they raise the price of hats instead of cutting the price of beaver.
[54]The price set in 1749 was three livres, ten sols, for both fat and dry prime beaver. In 1750 this price was further reduced by five sols. The war prices were discontinued on August 21, 1749. Abstract of Despatches in *Doc. Rel. to the Col. Hist. of N. Y.*, X, 199 ff.

decided decline in the prices of the common trade goods from 1740 to 1744. This is chiefly explained in the fact that government purchases at the western posts for the Chickasaw campaign of 1739-1740 and later forays had created an unusual scarcity of available goods at the beginning of this period. Then followed a gradual decline in prices as traders' stocks were replaced. The outbreak of war with the English, however, caused an immediate rise of something like forty per cent in the price of goods at the western posts, and this trend was aggravated as the war continued. By 1747 it was almost impossible to obtain goods for the trade, due to the English control of the seas, and of the 10,000 ells of cloth received in 1746 much was lost in a fire in the Quebec storehouse.[55] The return of peace brought relief from this situation, but it is certain that prices did not return to the pre-war level.

The war also brought goods of a poorer quality. We have mention of kettles of the wrong shape and size being sent to the Illinois country, and references to the poor quality of *écarlatines* are common.[56]

It must not be concluded, however, that the English were able to take full advantage of the French embarrassment in regard to the western trade. Though Oswego was drawing a considerable trade in beavers from the western country, as early as 1744 the Iroquois began to complain of the increasing price of goods there, alleging that merchandise was so dear that they found no advantage in trading with the English.[57] The presence of French raiding parties in the general vicinity of Oswego in the period from 1746 to 1748 probably reduced English trade in that area to a minimum. By 1749, however, the English were again plying a thriving trade at this post.[58] As for the trade in the Hudson Bay region, the French are said to have traded at this time on terms equal with if not better than those of the English.[59]

The decade closed with the French redoubling their efforts to strengthen their trade with the savages. A new post was built at Toronto in 1749 and a military expedition sent into the Ohio valley. An ordinance was issued in May, 1750, "to put an end to the infringements of the prohibitions inserted in the licenses, to prevent the farmers and voyageurs encroaching upon one another's rights, to stop the coureurs de bois, to forbid the trade carried on by certain voyageurs with the English, and finally to divert the savage nations from the said trade." The traders were exhorted to follow all regulations carefully, and convoys were to

---

[55]Hocquart to Minister, Quebec, Sept. 18, 1746, *Arch. Nat., Col.*, C^{11}A, 85:312^v-315^v.
[56]See, for instance, Vaudreuil to Minister, New Orleans, Oct. 30, 1745, *Ibid.*, C^{13}A, 29:91-91^v.
[57]Complaints made at the Albany Council, 1744, 1745, in *N. Y. Hist. Soc. Coll.*, 1869, 512-522.
[58]See returns of trade at Oswego for 1749 as given in *Doc. Rel. to the Col. Hist. of N. Y.*, VI, 538. According to this source 1,385 packets of furs, valued at 21,406 pounds, were received, these furs coming for the most part from western Indians.
[59]*House of Commons, Report*, 1749, 216 ff.

THE FUR TRADE 63

be put under military command.[60] With the benefits accruing from closer trade regulation, with a firm control of the Ohio region, and with the possibilities of extending the trade area farther to the northwest through such ventures as that of the La Vérendryes, it seemed not unlikely that the French beaver trade could be made secure against English competition.

[60]La Jonquière to Minister, Sept. 29, 1750, *Wisc. Hist. Coll.*, XVIII, 70-73. The post at Toronto was garrisoned by fifteen soldiers and was intended to intercept the flow of trade to the English across the lake. The expedition of Céloron to the Ohio was sent to warn the English and Indians of French intentions, while at the same time the construction of a post or posts in that area was being considered. Abstract of Despatches, 1749, *Doc. Rel. to the Col. Hist. of N. Y.*, X, 202; Minister to La Jonquière, April 15, 1750, *Can. Arch. Rep.*, 1905, I, 132.

Chapter IV

GENERAL INDIAN RELATIONS

THE CHIEF CONCERN of the French in regard to their power in the western country was their relations with the several Indian tribes. "Of all the divisions of the administration intrusted to the Sieur de la Jonquière, that which demands the most particular cares to be exercised on his part is the administration of the Indians . . . ."[1] This is a typical statement of the minister in issuing instructions to a new governor. Under Indian administration, the French recognized three groups of savages: (1) Indians who were domiciliated at the posts of the western country, (2) those domiciliated near the larger cities of Canada, and (3) the free Indians, who ranged the woods beyond immediate control. The following Indian settlements had been formed near the larger Canadian towns: (1) at Lorette, near Quebec, was a village of Huron; (2) at Bécancourt and St. Francis, near Three Rivers, were two villages comprised of Abenaki; (3) at the Sault St. Louis and the Lake of the Two Mountains, near Montreal, were located two villages, the one of Iroquois, and the other of Iroquois, Algonkin, and Nepissing; and (4) a sixth village was founded in 1749 near the north end of Lake Champlain, called Missikoui, which was attracting Delaware, Abenaki, and some others.

Each of these villages, excepting those at the Lake of the Two Mountains and at Missikoui, was served by a Jesuit missionary; the Sulpicians conducted missions at the other two places. These villages were closely allied to the French, had accepted their religion, and had become entirely dependent upon them for protection against enemies and famine. In turn, they assisted the French in offensive and defensive war and usually favored them with their trade. The Indians domiciliated about the posts as a rule did not embrace the Christian religion (with the exception of the Huron at Detroit and the Illinois tribes) and were much less closely bound to the French than those domiciliated near the larger settlements. Their policy was sometimes at one with that of their more savage neighbors, but generally they were subject to French control. In regard to the free tribes of the forest or prairie, the French sought to control them as far as possible by exploiting their trade and keeping peace between them and the domiciliated Indians.[2]

Each spring, usually in May, the governor of Canada met the deputies of the savages at Montreal (the Louisiana governor met the southern tribes at Mobile in like manner). In council meetings he sought to impress

---
[1] Instructions to La Jonquière, Apr. 1, 1746, *Arch. Nat., Col.*, B, 83:28ᵛ.
[2] Royal Instructions to La Jonquière, 1749, Versailles, *Ibid.*, B, 89:51ᵛ-52.

his will upon them, to direct their actions toward his interest, and more specifically to encourage them to give their trade to the French. At the close of the conference, presents were distributed. Merchants also took advantage of this occasion to trade with the Indians, for many of them brought down furs.[3] Sometimes the governor spent as much as three months at Montreal busied with affairs of Indian diplomacy.[4] In the Indian administration, the post commandant held a very important place, for his was much of the responsibility incident to direct contact with the savages. Besides being an officer of ordinary talents, he must also be a diplomat of first rank.[5] In this regard the missionary was also often very helpful.

Our task here is to note the operation of French policy in regard to the Indian tribes as well as to discuss the outstanding diplomatic problems of the period. Some of these are discussed in detail to give the reader an idea of the operation of the system itself.

The Huron at Detroit presented one of the chief problems to the French. This tribe was small, numbering only about two hundred men; however, the Huron were a very spirited people, and were ill at ease among the Ottawa, who hated them sincerely.[6] The trouble between these two tribes was probably of long standing, but the fact that the Huron had lately refused to make war on the Chickasaw was the immediate cause for the quarrel. Inasmuch as the Ottawa were still heathen, they also despised the Huron because they were "praying Indians." A solution to the problem might be found in moving the Huron to some other site, but this was always dangerous because it might antagonize other nations or otherwise go against French interests. The Huron were said to be thinking of moving to the Ohio valley, where it was feared they might come under English influence. A rumor was also current in 1739 that they would join themselves to some southern tribe. At the same time, they had asked to be removed to the region of Montreal.[7] Throughout 1740, they negotiated with Beauharnois through the Detroit commandant and La Richardie, the missionary. Nicolas, one of the head chiefs, seemed in favor of this move, but Anguirot, a notorious drunkard, was opposed to it. Shortly afterwards, Nicolas showed his real temper by withdrawing with a considerable following. He led his people to Sandusky on the south shore of Lake Erie where he established a village.[8]

---
[3]Instructions to La Jonquière, Apr. 1, 1746, *Ibid.*, B, 83:29-29ᵛ. Of course, the Indians brought gifts to the governor, the exchange of gifts being an important part of diplomatic proceedings. Fine fur robes are commonly mentioned among gifts of the savages. Indian diplomacy is a subject requiring special consideration, and will not be treated in the scope of this essay. For a vivid description of how it was conducted, see "Canada, Memoir on the Indian Nations, 1742," *Ibid.*, C¹¹A, 78:388-392.
[4]Beauharnois to Minister, Quebec, Aug. 14, 1742, *Ibid.*, C¹¹A, 77:83-84.
[5]Instructions to La Jonquière, Apr. 1, 1746, *Ibid.*, B, 83:78ᵛ.
[6]Memoir on Indians, Apr., 1741, *Ibid.*, C¹¹A, 76:315-317ᵛ.
[7]Unsigned Memorandum on Indian Affairs at Detroit, 1738-1741, Cadillac Papers, *Mich. Pion. and Hist. Coll.*, 34, 195 ff.
[8]*Ibid.* Armand de la Richardie (1686-1758) served at the Detroit mission from 1728 to his death, excepting 1746-1747 when he was recalled by the governor.

While this matter was under consideration, the minister insisted that a change of commandants be made at the post. It was thought that De Noyelle lacked influence with the nations, hence his failure to reassure the Huron. Although Beauharnois was not pleased with the appointment of De Noyan, the new commandant, he could only acquiesce in it.[9] We shall have occasion later to see how this factor was to operate during Beauharnois' attempt to remove the Huron to Montreal.

Another important factor is the attitude of La Richardie, who in 1739-1740 spent some time at the new Huron settlement which was forming at Sandusky, supposedly attempting to persuade those people to return to Detroit. At this time he began to oppose the plan of removing the tribe to Sault St. Louis on the excuse that the enmity of one of the Iroquois chiefs there would make it inadvisable.[10] The real reason for La Richardie's opposition is found in his jealousy of the Sulpicians who had charge of the mission at the Lake of the Two Mountains. Even though the Huron were asked to settle at the Sault where the Jesuits were in control, it was quite likely that they would prefer the Lake region.[11] De Noyelle, too, had opposed the whole movement, and was confident that he could solve the problem by getting the Huron to re-enter the war against the Chickasaw, in which case their enemies would cease to press them at Detroit.[12]

In spite of the above-mentioned opposition, the governor was sanguine for the removal. He had conceived the idea of replacing the Huron at Detroit with the Shawnee from the Ohio country. This would solve both the Huron problem and that of the Shawnee, who because of their commercial relations with the English were being led away from French allegiance.[13] Beauharnois, therefore, decided to attempt to remove the Huron to the vicinity of Montreal, and he chose his nephew, the Chevalier de Beauharnois, to lead them.[14]

In the summer of 1741, the Chevalier, accompanied by four aides and two canoes of the domiciliated Iroquois, set out for Detroit.[15] On August 2, he delivered the governor's message to the Huron, finding them reluctant to leave.[16] In the first place, the Huron had largely returned to

---

[9]Minister to Beauharnois, Versailles, May 2, 1740, *Arch. Nat., Col.,* B, 70:342-342ᵛ; Minister to De Noyan, May 2, 1740, *Ibid.,* B, 70:349-349ᵛ. De Noyan evidently had influence at the court which secured his appointment against the governor's wishes.
[10]Beauharnois to Minister, Quebec, Oct. 1, 1740, *Ibid.,* C¹¹A, 74:80-84.
[11]Extract from Letter of La Richardie to St. Pé, Detroit, Aug. 26, 1740, *Ibid.,* C¹¹A, 74:268-269ᵛ.
[12]Beauharnois to Minister, Quebec, Oct. 1, 1740, *Ibid.,* C¹¹A, 74:80-84.
[13]Memoir on Indians, 1741, *Ibid.,* C¹¹A, 76:315-317ᵛ. The king approved this policy also. Minister to Beauharnois, Marly, May 6, 1741, *Ibid.,* B, 72:373-374.
[14]Beauharnois to Minister, Quebec, Oct. 1, 1741, *Ibid.,* C¹¹A, 74:80-84. See also instructions to the Chevalier, in *Wisc. Hist. Coll.,* XVII, 346-348. Beauharnois also prepared the Indians at the Sault and the Lake to receive the Huron, persuading them to agree to this by a liberal distribution of presents. Words of Beauharnois to the Iroquois of the Sault and Lake, June 12, 1741, *Arch. Nat., Col.,* C¹¹A, 75:106-109. Three hundred *minots* of flour, one hundred and fifty of corn, and forty-five of peas were distributed at this time. Claude de Beauharnois (1717-?) was a nephew of the governor, and a captain in the army. His choice for this mission could be defended by reason of his being an adopted chief in the villages at the Sault and Lake.
[15]See expense account for the equipment of his party, *Arch. Nat., Col.,* C¹¹A, 76:227-239.
[16]*Ibid.,* C¹¹A, 75:99-99ᵛ.

the war against the Chickasaw.[17] The opposition of the chief, Anguirot, whom the Chevalier described as an "accomplished politician" was also a considerable factor. Then, too, he soon became aware of La Richardie's lack of cooperation. The Chevalier also complained that he had no presents suitable for the Huron women, whom he described as being held in high esteem by their men.[18]

After spending a month at Detroit without accomplishing anything, the Chevalier went to Sandusky to see what could be done there. Though La Richardie went along, he tells us that he gave the Chevalier little assistance in the accomplishment of his purpose.[19] At the same time he wrote his superior, giving an exaggerated account of the success of the Jesuit mission at Detroit, hoping thereby to influence him in opposing the removal of the Huron.[20] Finally, the Chevalier was forced to return to Montreal, accompanied by only a few old Huron chiefs. Beauharnois could only ask for the minister's approval of the course he had taken.[21]

The failure of the Chevalier's mission determined the governor to take revenge on La Richardie, as well as on the others who had opposed him. He had taken the opportunity to seize some of the father's letters from which he had gleaned the information we have noted above. In 1742, Beauharnois wrote: "The conduct which the chiefs have shown toward my nephew has not come of their own part; it has been aroused in them by their missionary." La Richardie was accused not only of thwarting the governor's plans, but also of encouraging the Huron to remove to another location near Detroit. In general, the governor charged that the Jesuits were trying to get control of the government,[22] and he made so bold as to hint that La Richardie may have been under English influence. Accordingly orders were issued which removed the Jesuit from the mission.[23] In this, however, the governor was thwarted for the time being, for the priest sent to relieve La Richardie feigned sickness, and returned, leaving La Richardie in charge of the mission for some time.[24]

Beauharnois' attitude toward De Noyan was quite as antagonistic. De Noyan in self-defense corresponded directly with the minister, and laid

---

[17]The Chevalier says over one hundred and sixty warriors were out on this mission at that time. This compares very closely with information drawn from Detroit expense accounts.
[18]Chevalier de Beauharnois to the Marquis de Beauharnois, Detroit, Aug. 2, 1741, *Wisc. Hist. Coll.*, XVII, 353-355.
[19]Father de La Richardie to Father de Jaunay, Detroit, Dec., 1741, *Arch. Nat., Col.*, C¹¹A, 75:124-124ᵛ. At this time La Richardie feared the governor intended to remove the Huron to the new village being founded by the Sulpician, Piquet, at the head of Lake Champlain. The expense accounts at Detroit show that La Richardie was greatly interested in selling supplies to the Chevalier, and even rented him a house for lodging. The Missionary's smith also did considerable work for the party.
[20]La Richardie to the Father General, June 21, 1741, Thwaites, *Jes. Rel.*, 69, 51-53. He did not, however, favor the plan of getting the Huron to go back to war with the Chickasaw, having scruples against such action. La Richardie to Father St. Pé, Detroit, June 10, 1741, *Wisc. Hist. Coll.*, XVII, 339-340.
[21]Beauharnois to Minister, Quebec, Sept. 20, 1742, *Arch. Nat., Col.*, C¹¹A, 77:106-107.
[22]Beauharnois to Minister, Quebec, Sept. 15, 1742, *Ibid.*, C¹¹A, 75:121-125ᵛ. Also same to same, Nov. 12, 1742, *Wisc. Hist. Coll.*, XVII, 431; *Arch. Nat., Col.*, C¹¹A, 75:249-250.
[23]Beauharnois to Minister, Sept. 17, 1743, Quebec, *Ibid.*, C¹¹A, 79:110-110ᵛ.
[24]Beauharnois to Minister, Quebec, Oct. 9, 1744, *Ibid.*, C¹¹A, 81:160ᵛ-161. La Richardie really did not leave Detroit until 1746.

his grievances before him. He did not deny that he had opposed Beauharnois in the attempt to remove the Huron, but he claimed he had done so because he had seen the impracticability of the governor's plan. In 1741 he wrote that the measures being taken to eradicate illicit trade with the English about the post were having such good results that this evil had nearly disappeared. It was his opinion that the money Beauharnois had spent in trying to remove the Huron would have done far more good had it been spent for presents for the nations about the post. He also complained that Beauharnois tried to rule Detroit from Quebec, and that Hocquart wanted to set up a sub-delegate there who would take away the commandant's legal powers.[25] As De Noyan saw it, Beauharnois, in sending his nephew to Detroit, had sought to rob the commandant of his usual powers of directing Indian movements about the post. However, he did not wish to have it appear that he had actually worked against the Chevalier in the negotiations at Detroit. Rather he ascribed the failure to the inconstancy of the savages, the *rapprochement* with the Ottawa, and the distrust of the Huron for the Iroquois at the Sault. He agreed that the return of the Huron to war with the Chickasaw was an additional reason. In spite of De Noyan's connections with the court, Beauharnois was strong enough to remove him from his command.[26] Hocquart also opposed the governor in this matter, talking to him "freely" on the subject. His main objection seems to have been the cost of removing the tribe, which he estimated would be more than 100,000 livres.[27]

Beauharnois had now decided to abandon plans to remove the Huron. It seems that he had reached this conclusion while the Chevalier was still on his mission.[28] The minister accordingly gave his approval that the Huron should remain at Detroit.[29] As for the Huron, they were now going against the Chickasaw, and the young men appeared satisfied, though rumors circulated that their interest in the war had begun to lag.[30] When Céloron reached Detroit, he found them quite restless, and he feared momentarily that they would remove toward the south of the Ohio.[31] Finally in 1743 the Huron, with a few Pottawattomie and others, settled at the place called *La Grande Terre* just below Detroit and gave no more trouble until the outbreak of 1747.[32] Most of the party at

---

[25] De Noyan to Minister, Detroit, Aug. 24, 1741, *Wisc. Hist. Coll.*, XVII, 356 ff. De Noyan evidently preferred to have his superiors in Paris rather than nearer at home.
[26] De Noyan to Minister, Detroit, Aug. 20, 1742. *Arch. Nat., Col.*, C¹¹A, 78:248-254ᵛ. For the removal of De Noyan, see Beauharnois to Minister, Sept. 15, 1742, *Ibid.*, C¹¹A, 75:121-125ᵛ. Céloron succeeded him (1742).
[27] Hocquart to Minister, June 11, 1742, *Ibid.*, C¹¹A, 77:277-283. In the same letter, he reveals also that he had corresponded with La Richardie on the subject—this doubtless being unknown to Beauharnois. Beauharnois and Hocquart were on bad terms at this time.
[28] Beauharnois to Minister, Quebec, Oct. 8, 1741, *Wisc. Hist. Coll.*, XVII, 369-370. Beauharnois to the Three Huron Chiefs, June 28, 1742, *Ibid.*, 377-380.
[29] Minister to Beauharnois, Versailles, Feb. 14, 1742, *Arch. Nat., Col.*, B, 74:413.
[30] *Petite Mémoire de Canada*, 1742, *Ibid.*, C¹¹A, 78:318ᵛ.
[31] Beauharnois to Minister, Quebec, Sept. 15, 1742, *Ibid.*, C¹¹A, 75:125-125ᵛ. Memoir on Indians, January, 1743, *Ibid.*, C¹¹A, 80:361.
[32] Minister to Beauharnois, Versailles, Mar. 30, 1744, *Ibid.*, B, 78:340; Beauharnois to Minister, Quebec, Oct. 9, 1744, *Ibid.*, C¹¹A, 81:160-160ᵛ. This location was on the north side of the river, near the present Sandwich, Ontario.

Sandusky remained there in spite of French attempts to entice them back to Detroit.[33] The Ottawa at Michilimakinac presented a problem similar to that of the Huron at Detroit. This tribe numbered only about two hundred and fifty warriors, but like the Huron they were restless and wanted to move.[34] Their restlessness was not due to pressure from enemies; indeed, we find them working in perfect harmony with the Pottawattomie in 1740 to "cover the death" of a Frenchman killed by a Sauteur boy at that time.[35] They claimed they sought better lands for their crops, though the fact that the French had had some trouble with one of their chiefs, Pendalouan, seems more likely to have caused dissatisfaction in the tribe. This chief had distinguished himself in war with the Foxes, and had worn the governor's medal, but in 1740 he had grown insolent and had given his medal to another chief. Though the rest of the tribe had disavowed him in this act, he still retained much influence with his people.[36]

In any case, the tribe determined to move, and started for the Wisconsin region. Not being able to restrain them from this act, Céloron, then commandant at Michilimakinac, went along with them. They spent the winter of 1740-1741 in that country, probably on the Mississippi. In the spring, the French officer succeeded in getting most of them to return to Michilimakinac.[37] When the Ottowa deputies went to Montreal that spring, the governor discussed their problem with them, trying to direct their removal to some place near the post so that they would not become a threat to the French in the west by going near the English. He was also anxious that their trade at Michilimakinac should not be lost. At a council in July, Beauharnois pointed out to them two locations which he had selected, the choice of one being left to their own decision.[38]

They returned undecided, and Céloron fell to work helping them to extend their clearings near the fort, hoping this might encourage them to stay where they were.[39] They indicated, however, that they would soon make a choice between the two locations selected by the governor, promis-

---

[33]Words of Kinonsaki, Ottawa chief, to the Sandusky Hurons, May 5, 1743, *Ibid.*, C¹¹A, 79:95-96; Beauharnois to Minister, Sept. 17, 1743, *Ibid.*, C¹¹A, 79:108ᵛ-110. The whereabouts of Nicolas' village after 1747 is a mystery. It was thought he had moved toward *La Demoiselle's* village on the Miami or farther eastward. Bonnécamps says they found no trace of him in 1749, but heard he was on the Lake. We know Nicolas died sometime during 1750. See report of his death in La Jonquière to Minister, Quebec, Oct. 10, 1750, *Wisc. Hist. Coll.*, XVIII, 71-75.
[34]See Johnson's estimation of Indian numbers made in 1763 in Pouchot, *op. cit.*, II, 260.
[35]Beauharnois to Minister, Quebec, Oct. 2, 1740, *Arch. Nat., Col.*, C¹¹A, 74:13-14.
[36]Beauharnois to Minister, Quebec, Oct. 3, 1740, *Ibid.*, C¹¹A, 74:21-22. See also the disavowal of Pendalouan by the Ottawa chiefs, Aug. 7, 1740, *Ibid.*, C¹¹A, 74:25. This is attached to the governor's letter of October 3rd.
[37]Same to same, Quebec, Oct. 5, 1741, *Ibid.*, C¹¹A, 75:201-203.
[38]They had later attempted to go to the valley of the Muskegon River in the present state of Michigan, not, however, with French approval. The two places chosen by the governor were Pouchetaoucy, at the extremity of Bay St. Ignace at the head of Lake Huron, and *L'Arbre Croche*, or the Crooked Tree, which was located on the northwest corner of the Michigan Peninsula. Locations given by O'Callaghan, *Doc. Rel. to the Col. Hist. of N. Y.*, IX, 1072.
[39]Céloron to Beauharnois, Sept. 2, 1741, *Wisc. Hist. Coll.*, XVII, 359-360. From expense accounts we learn that the savages were given seed corn in liberal amounts at this time. A serious shortage of grain then existed there. In 1742 corn sold at twenty-five livres per sack. After the harvest of that year, the price fell to fifteen livres. The soil at Michilimakinac was not good for agriculture.

ing to do this before the following spring. They were encouraged in this by continued promises of the French that they would have access to more brandy at Montreal than they had been used to having, while Pendalouan, now anxious to be restored to the favor of the governor, gave the benefit of his influence.[40] The persistence of Céloron, aided by the influence of Pendalouan, finally won out, and in the spring of 1742, the tribe moved to *L'Arbre Croche,* where the French commandant "lighted their fire."[41] Barring minor disturbances with the Sioux, the Ottawa gave no further trouble during this period. Pendalouan went before the governor in 1742, and was pardoned for his past misdemeanors.[42]

The Sac and Foxes had given the French no serious trouble since the Fox War, though they had remained under suspicion.[43] In 1739, Beauharnois sent out to the Wisconsin area Sieur Marin, a skillful trader and Indian agent, who was ordered to lead the Sac and Foxes back to *La Baye* where they were to be permanently settled. This would serve to increase the trade at that post, while the machinations of these tribes with the western Sioux would be curbed.[44] The Foxes had begun to press toward the Illinois, and had recently killed a French deserter from that post, supposedly by mistake.[45] In the spring of 1739, Marin tried to persuade the Bay chiefs to go to Montreal to confer with the governor, but succeeded in getting only two Sioux and one Winnebago to follow him.[46] Although the Sioux seemed repentant, during the summer of 1739 they fell upon a group of Ottawa and killed them. They excused themselves by blaming the Foxes, whom they accused of having spread abroad rumors that the Ottawa had attacked the Sioux chiefs who were returning from Montreal.[47] Marin, in spite of the government's suspicions, thought the Sioux could be won over by conciliation. To accomplish this, he deemed it essential that a trading post be built on the upper Mississippi, but the king disapproved.[48]

In 1740, Marin brought down the chiefs of the Sac, Foxes, Winnebago, Ottawa, and *Folles Avoines,* but no Sioux, for they would not come after their stroke on the Ottawa the summer before. Discussions held with these disclosed that they were all favorably inclined to peace, though the French were careful not to mention to the Foxes the murder of the

---

[40]Beauharnois to Minister, Quebec, Oct. 5, 1741, *Arch. Nat., Col.,* C¹¹A, 75:201-203ᵛ; Minister to Beauharnois, Versailles, Apr. 20, 1742, *Ibid.,* B, 74:468-469ᵛ.
[41]The Ottawa at Montreal, June 16, 1742, *Wisc. Hist. Coll.,* XVII, 372-373.
[42]Beauharnois to Minister, Quebec, May 12, 1741, *Arch. Nat., Col.,* C¹¹E, 16:237-239ᵛ; same to same, Quebec, Sept. 24, 1742, *Ibid.,* C¹¹A, 77:108-112ᵛ. He was not restored just then to his full dignities, but Beauharnois recommended this in 1744. Same to same, Oct. 13, 1743, Quebec, *Ibid.,* C¹¹A, 79:173ᵛ-174.
[43]Memoir on Indians, 1738, *Ibid.,* C¹¹A, 70:257-259.
[44]Beauharnois to Minister, Montreal, June 30, 1739, *Ibid.,* C¹¹A, 71:35-35ᵛ.
[45]Memoir on Canada, 1740, *Ibid.,* C¹¹A, 74:232-236ᵛ.
[46]*Ibid.*
[47]Words of the chiefs to Marin, Mar. 9, 1740, *Ibid.,* C¹¹A, 74:85-85ᵛ.
[48]Memoir of the King to Beauharnois and Hocquart, Marly, May 13, 1740, *Ibid.,* B, 70:359-363ᵛ.

Frenchman in 1739.[49] Beauharnois contented himself with encouraging the others to keep peace with the Sioux—a delicate business, since the Sioux were rampant in that country.[50] The savages returned in a better mood, loaded with presents. Then, too, they were well received by the Ottawa as they passed by Michilimakinac.[51]

However, the controversy which had arisen between the Sioux and the northern tribes required additional attention. Marin finally went to Chequamigon to attend to this matter, where he held conferences with the Sauteur and others in which he succeeded in pacifying them.[52] This work was also important for the well-being of the French trade in that region.[53] Nevertheless, secret alliances and combinations were concocted by the Sauteur and others against the Sioux, and some parties were actually sent out against them, especially by the Ottawa who smarted from the blow of 1739.[54]

The Sioux, also, were suspected of planning attacks on the Illinois, but seem to have been diverted somewhat by the troubles with the northern Indians.[55] Nevertheless, attacks were made by either Sioux or Foxes on the Illinois in 1740, two of the latter being slain.[56] To avenge the deaths of their people, the Illinois sent an expedition of sixty men into the Wisconsin country. Upon their reaching the mouth of the Wisconsin River, the Illinois halted, being uncertain as to whether to attack the Sioux or the Foxes. Meeting by chance with some of the latter, they fell upon them and slew four women. When the Sac heard of this affair, they in turn fell upon the Illinois who were returning home via the Mississippi, killing nine and taking five. They claimed this attack was made by mistake, contending that they had taken the Illinois for Missouri Indians.[57] This affair increased Beauharnois' suspicions against the Foxes, whom he also accused of having "underground belts" with the English. He considered using the forces he had gathered at that time for an attack on Oswego, to make war on the Foxes. Longueuil and other western officers were said to be in sympathy with this idea, and it was certain the court would approve, especially since it was disclosed that the Foxes were planning to seek refuge among the Iroquois or the Sioux.[58]

[49]Marin said he had not been able to do anything about it because of illness, and Beauharnois passed over the matter on the theory that it is better to let sleeping dogs lie. Beauharnois to Minister, Oct. 1, 1740, *Wisc. Hist. Coll.*, XVII, 329-330. Memoir on Indians, 1741, *Arch. Nat., Col.*, C¹¹A, 76:315-317ᵛ.
[50]Responses of the Sac, Foxes, et al., July 5, 1740, *Ibid.*, C¹¹A, 74:60-61.
[51]Beauharnois to Minister, Quebec, Oct. 15, 1740, *Ibid.*, C¹¹A, 114:139-139ᵛ.
[52]Extensive conferences were held there in September, 1741. See expense accounts, *Ibid.*, C¹¹A, 75:286-287.
[53]Margry, VI, 653.
[54]Beauharnois to Minister, Quebec, Aug. 14, 1742, *Arch. Nat., Col.*, C¹¹A, 77:83-84; Oct. 12, 1742, *Ibid.*, C¹¹E, 16:251-265ᵛ.
[55]Minister to Bienville, Fontainebleau, Oct. 25, 1740, *Ibid.*, B, 70:466-466ᵛ.
[56]Bienville to Minister, New Orleans, Apr. 30, 1741, *Ibid.*, C¹³A, 26:81-87; Benoist de St. Clair to Salmon, Dec. 5, 1740, *Ibid.*, C¹³A, 26:143-144. Benoist thought the enemy were Foxes.
[57]Beauharnois to Minister, Quebec, Sept. 26, 1741, *Wisc. Hist. Coll.*, XVII, 365-366.
[58]Abstract of Despatches, *Doc. Rel. to the Col. Hist. of N. Y.*, IX, 1085-1086.

In the meanwhile Marin was still working on his project to solve the problem by returning the Sac and Foxes to their old homes at *La Baye*. In furtherance of this policy, the governor had issued an order that no traders from the Illinois should trade with those tribes under penalty of being declared *coureurs de bois*.[59] Although the Sioux had promised Marin to go down to Montreal in 1741, they had become so embroiled with their neighbors that it was impossible to get them to do anything. Then, too, a strong party of Sauteur went against them at that time, several of the Sioux being slain. The Sioux themselves killed a Frenchman in the Wisconsin region.[60] In spite of these embroilments, Marin came down in 1742, accompanied by two Sioux chiefs, one of whom was the influential Ouakantapé. He was also accompanied by goodly representations from the Sac, Foxes, Winnebago, *Folles Avoines*, and Sauteur of Chequamigon.[61] During parleys with the governor, the Sioux asked for peace, pleading heavy losses at the hands of their enemies. The Sac and Foxes said their people had almost all returned to *La Baye*, while the Winnebago also reported that a large part of their people had returned there. The governor restored to the Sioux four of their slaves and ordered two more who had been taken in 1741[62] to be delivered to them. He thought this kindness on his part of restoring their lost people would serve to keep them quiet.[63]

Marin, though still under the suspicion of the minister, returned to his charge, Beauharnois pleading his merit, and pointing out that Marin had promised the Indians to return with them.[64] Upon the return of the Sioux to Michilimakinac, De Verchères delivered to them two other slaves as promised. Here, too, a conference was held between the Bay Indians and the Ottawa, the results of which were promising.[65] That the Sioux were earnest in their desire for peace is shown by the fact that though the Sauteur made new raids on them in the autumn of 1742, they did not retaliate.[66] In November, Marin conferred with large numbers of both the Prairie and Lake Sioux who expressed themselves in terms of warmest affection for the French, and promised to go to see "Onontio" in

---

[59]The Sac and Foxes were located on the Rock River in Wisconsin. The governor's policy of trying to give Marin a monopoly of trade there may have a different interpretation. Marin was already under the minister's censure for his trading activities. Was the governor also interested in this trade? See Beauharnois to Minister, Sept. 26, 1741, *Wisc. Hist. Coll.*, XVII, 362-364.
[60]Beauharnois to Minister, Sept. 26, 1741, *Wisc. Hist. Coll.*, XVII, 360-362; Minister to Beauharnois, Versailles, Apr. 20, 1742, *Arch. Nat., Col.*, B, 74:468-469ᵛ.
[61]Beauharnois to Minister, Quebec, Aug. 14, 1742, *Ibid.*, C¹¹A, 77:83-84.
[62]These prisoners had been taken in the war between the Monsonis, a tribe located near Rainy Lake, and the Sioux. La Vérendrye's skillful diplomacy had brought peace to this region after 1742.
[63]Beauharnois to Minister, Quebec, Sept. 24, 1742, *Ibid.*, C¹¹A, 77:108-112ᵛ.
[64]*Ibid.*
[65]Beauharnois to Minister, Quebec, Oct. 12, 1742, *Ibid.*, C¹¹E, 16:258-265ᵛ. Jean Jarret, Sieur de Vercheres (1687-1752) was a brother of the famous Madeleine. He commanded at *La Baye* in 1747 and at Frontenac in 1732.
[66]Beauharnois to Minister, Quebec, Sept. 24, 1742, *Ibid.*, C¹¹A, 77:108-112ᵛ; Oct. 12, 1742, *Ibid.*, C¹¹E, 16:258-265ᵛ.

GENERAL INDIAN RELATIONS 73

the spring. By this time the governor had also succeeded in restoring peace between the Foxes and the *Folles Avoines* and between the Sac and the Illinois.[67] In spite of these successes, Marin was still under the suspicion of the minister, and his recall was inevitable. Charges were made against him, both on grounds of lack of ability, and of working too much "in affairs that regard his own interests."[68] These charges finally resulted in his recall in 1742, the minister being of the opinion that the Sac and Foxes could not be returned to *La Baye*.[69] Marin returned in 1743, bringing down a considerable deputation of the Sioux. Beauharnois did what he could to justify him and to allow him to return to France on business. He was succeeded by Sieur de Lusignan.[70]

News now came that the Sioux in spite of seemingly good intentions were seeking a direct alliance with the Foxes—a policy which seemed a very detrimental one to the French. This report drew from the minister an order to prevent the movement.[71] Beauharnois at once took issue with the minister in regard to this policy because he believed it impossible to prevent the alliance. Additional reasons for his opposition are found in his pique against the minister over the removal of Marin and also his jealousy of Bienville who had proposed the policy. In a carefully formed letter, he showed his superior that he could do no better than to rely upon the peaceful demonstrations made by both Sioux and Foxes, for the attempt to separate them could only mean war, which he knew the colony was not in condition to undertake. He also pointed out that the Foxes and Sac had now returned to *La Baye* with the exception of about a dozen cabins located near the south end of the lake.[72] The minister could only acquiesce in Beauharnois' policy. It is a good example of how the French autocracy could be thwarted by a determined governor.[73]

By 1743, La Vérendrye had the more distant tribes well under control, and had received from them promises that they would not attack the Sioux for two years. La Corne Dubreuil, working at Kamanistiquia, had carried out a similar policy in the vicinity of his post.[74] In general,

---
[67]See words of the Sioux to Marin, Nov. 18, Nov. 24, 1742, *Ibid.*, C¹¹A, 79:120-121ᵛ; Memoir on Indians, Jan., 1743, *Ibid.*, C¹¹A, 80:359ᵛ-360. The Indians called the governor "Onontio."
[68]Minister to Beauharnois, Marly, May 6, 1741, *Ibid.*, B, 72:373-374.
[69]Same to same, Versailles, Apr. 20, 1742, *Ibid.*, B, 74:468-469ᵛ.
[70]Beauharnois to Minister, Quebec, Nov. 2, 1742, *Ibid.*, C¹¹A, 75:243-243ᵛ; Oct. 13, 1743, Quebec, *Ibid.*, C¹¹A, 79:176ᵛ-177; Words of the Bay chiefs and Response of Marin, Apr. 25, 1743, *Ibid.*, C¹¹A, 79:126-127.
[71]Bienville to Minister, New Orleans, Feb. 4, 1743, *Ibid.*, C¹³A, 28:33; Minister to Beauharnois, Versailles, May 31, 1743, *Ibid.*, B, 76:444-444ᵛ.
[72]Beauharnois to Minister, Sept. 18, 1743, Quebec, *Ibid.*, C¹¹A, 79:115-118ᵛ. These cabins were at *Chicagou* for the most part.
[73]Minister to Beauharnois, Versailles, Mar. 24, 1744, *Wisc. Hist. Coll.*, XVIII, 3-4.
[74]Beauharnois to Minister, Quebec, Sept. 17, 1743, *Arch. Nat., Col.*, C¹³A, 79:112-113ᵛ. François Josué de la Corne Dubreuil (1710-1754) held the office of commandant at Kamanistiquia in 1743. Pierre Gaultier de Varennes, Sieur de la Vérendrye (1685-1749), was given a concession to explore and trade in the region to the northwest of Lake Superior in 1731. He and his sons, during the next two decades, made extensive discoveries and opened up a new field for trade. Space does not permit a discussion of La Vérendrye's activities here, but good accounts may be found in G. M. Wrong, *The Rise and Fall of New France*, Vol. II, in Francis Parkman, *A Half Century of Conflict*, Vol. II, and in L. J. Burpee, *The Search for the Western Sea*.

quiet was restored in 1744, though minor outbreaks still occurred at intervals. Beauharnois hoped, upon the outbreak of the war with the English, to use the Indians about La Vérendrye's posts to make an attack on the English in the neighborhood of Hudson Bay. Such a campaign would release the pressure on the Sioux from the north, while it would react favorably among the other tribes about the Great Lakes as well.[75]

During the next two years, troubles arose at *La Baye* in which one Frenchman was killed. These irregularities were chiefly due, it seems, to the insolence of the *coureurs de bois* and troubles between the commandant and the traders.[76] Lusignan seems to have been unusually lax in dealing with the savages, for in 1745 when the Sioux killed three Frenchmen in the Illinois, he released the murderers when they were delivered to him, just as he had overlooked the death of the trader at *La Baye*.[77] However, quiet was soon restored, and it was not until the end of the decade that any further serious disturbances arose in the Wisconsin country, there being no trouble in that region even during the revolt of the western tribes in 1747. Marin was returned to the Sioux country in 1749, with orders to build a post among that nation, and to undertake explorations looking toward the discovery of the "western sea"—a project which the minister frowned upon as soon as he learned to whom its execution had been intrusted.[78]

At times the Indians on the Missouri created problems for the French at the Illinois. The number of these savages was not great, the Missouri possessing hardly 500 men and the Osage being much fewer.[79] Serious trouble arose in that region in 1740 when three Frenchmen were killed and several robbed of their goods. The Missouri also organized a war party against the Arkansas, allies of the French to the south.[80] Much of the trouble with these Indians, however, was due to abuses in the trade by *coureurs de bois* and other lawless elements. In 1741 Bienville ordered Sieur Benoist to send an officer and six men there to regulate the trade and keep down abuses. At the same time an attempt was made to scrutinize more closely the reputation of those who drew licenses for that trade.[81]

---

[75] Beauharnois to Minister, Quebec, Oct. 9, 1744, *Wisc. Hist. Coll.*, XVII, 441-442; Beauharnois to Minister, Quebec, Oct. 11, 1744, *Arch. Nat., Col.*, C11A, 81:166v. The expense accounts at Michilimakinac show that the Sauteur were actually subsidized to prevent them from going against the Sioux. For example, see *Ibid.*, C11A, 84:273-273v. At *La Baye* expenditures are found for such items as the purchase of slaves from the Sauteurs. La Vérendrye himself gave up two Sioux slaves he owned. See *Ibid.*, C11A, 117:357; *Ibid.*, C11A, 83:326.

[76] Beauharnois to Minister, Quebec, Oct. 28, 1746, *Doc. Rel. to the Col. Hist. of N. Y.*, X, 37-38. This matter is discussed under the fur trade, *supra*, pp. 54-55.

[77] Vaudreuil to Minister, New Orleans, Nov. 20, 1746, *Arch. Nat., Col.*, C13A, 30:71-72. A fourth Frenchman was killed at St. Philippe in the Illinois at about the same time. The Piankeshaw atoned for his death by delivering the head of the murderer's brother, not being able to take the murderer himself. Vaudreuil also says that the Foxes were put on good terms with the French by the surrender of some slaves taken from their nation and held in the Illinois.

[78] La Jonquière to Minister, Aug. 18, 1750, *Wisc. Hist. Coll.*, XVIII, 63-67; La Jonquière and Bigot to Minister, Quebec, Oct. 9, 1749, *Ibid.*, 33-34; Minister to La Jonquière and Bigot, Versailles, Apr. 15, 1750, *Ibid.*, 60-61.

[79] Memoir upon the State of the Colony of Louisiana in 1746, *Arch. Nat., Col.*, C13A, 30:258-259.

[80] Benoist de St. Clair to Salmon, July 28, 1740, *Ibid.*, C13A, 26:190-191.

[81] Bienville to Minister, Sept. 30, 1741, *Ibid.*, C13A, 26:97-106.

De Bertet, who was sent up to the Illinois command in 1742,[82] began to seek a solution to the problem, and a plan was eventually evolved which included farming out the Missouri trade to a trader who would undertake to support the French power there, as well as to extend exploration toward the southwest. Sieur Deruisseau, a Canadian *seigneur*, was granted this monopoly for five years beginning in 1745. He was obliged to build a fort, quarters for officers, barracks, a powder magazine, and a storehouse. He also undertook to pay the officer at the post a gratification of one hundred *pistoles* yearly, to transport the effects of the garrison from the Illinois, and to support them at his own expense. He was also expected to bear part of the expense of keeping the savages on good terms, even to the point of furnishing a part of the presents. It was expressly provided that no intoxicating liquor was to be sold to the savages; and the farmer was also enjoined to send all beaver, marten, and other fine skins to Canada, though all other produce might go to Louisiana.[83] Vaudreuil wrote in 1747 that the work on the fort and buildings was nearly finished; and De Bertet reported that the effect had been that of quelling the turmoils occasioned by the lawless elements in those parts.[84] Benoist, again in command at the Illinois after the death of De Bertet,[85] was faced with a new series of troubles in the Osage country, for these Indians had murdered two French *coureurs de bois*. Upon their sending chiefs to ask pardon for this act, it was thought best not to press the matter on account of the trouble it might entail.[86]

In regard to certain straggling elements of Nepissing and Algonkin, Beauharnois sought to congregate them at the Lake of the Two Mountains where he was preparing a village. This idea was associated with plans for the removal of the Huron from Detroit, and the migration of the Shawnee to that post to replace them. Of the three removals planned, only the settlement of the Nepissing and Algonkin was successful. Beauharnois estimated that he could gather from these roving tribes as many as 600 warriors, who, joined to the Iroquois and Detroit Huron (whom he then expected to come there), would make a bulwark at Montreal which would give full protection to the city from the south. This would also provide a strong potential force for offensive war against the English.[87] To facilitate the accomplishment of this project, he asked the minister for 15,000 livres, but only 2,000 livres per year were granted,

---
[82]Same to same, New Orleans, July 30, 1742, *Ibid.*, C¹³A, 27:84-84ᵛ.
[83]See *Mémoire* on this subject, Aug. 8, 1744, *Ibid.*, C¹³A, 28:226ᵛ-232. Minister to Vaudreuil, Versailles, Apr. 30, 1746, *Ibid.*, B, 83:15ᵛ-16.
[84]Vaudreuil to Minister, New Orleans, Mar. 15, 1747, *Ibid.*, C¹³A, 31:21-21ᵛ.
[85]De Bertet's death occurred Jan. 7, 1749.
[86]Vaudreuil to Minister, Aug. 26, 1749, *Arch. Nat., Col.*, C¹³A, 33:57-58; Minister to Vaudreuil, Sept. 26, 1750, *Ibid.*, B, 91:14. Benoist associated this new trouble to some extent with *La Demoiselle's* machinations. Benoist de St. Clair to De Raymond, Fort Chartres, Feb. 11, 1750, *Wisc. Hist. Coll.*, XVIII, 58-60.
[87]Beauharnois to Minister, May 12, 1741, *Arch. Nat., Col.*, C¹¹E, 16:237-239.

this to be taken out of fur trade revenues.[88] This subsidy was continued year after year, and Beauharnois soon reported that many of the vagabonds had been settled there.[89]

The Shawnee have been mentioned as presenting a problem to the French. This tribe, a remnant of the old Shawnee who once lived in Georgia were located on the Allegheny River near Pittsburgh. They were pro-French in sympathy, but much subject to English intrigue. Peter Chartier, a French half-breed, one of their most influential chiefs, had important trading connections with the English in Pennsylvania, and for some time the French had sought to remove the tribe to the west, where they could be better controlled. The French first planned to settle the tribe at Detroit, and later in the vicinity of the Miami post, but in 1745 the Shawnee suddenly migrated to the lower Ohio instead. They settled at the site of the modern Shawneetown, Illinois. The French were greatly embarrassed by this movement of the Shawnee, since they were unable at that time, due to the war conditions, to supply them with merchandise. As a result the Shawnee soon broke up, some of them moving southward to their kindred among the Alabama, and the others going up the Ohio to Scioto, where they joined with other savages, such as the Delaware, to form a center of English intrigue on the Ohio. The French thus lost their hold on the Shawnee, an event not without significance in the outcome of the struggle with the English for the control of the Ohio.[90]

In the early part of the decade, the French had experienced little trouble with the Indians who lived to the south and east of Lake Michigan. These tribes—the Wea, Kickapoo, Mascoutin, Piankeshaw, Pottawattomie, and Miami—were not strong in numbers,[91] and were generally docile, with the exception of the Miami.[92] At the conferences held at Montreal in July, 1742, Beauharnois was well pleased with the fidelity of these Indians, especially of the Kickapoo, Wea, and Mascoutin, who were taking an active part in the Chickasaw war.[93]

---

[88]Minister to Beauharnois, Apr. 20, 1742, *Ibid.*, B, 74:468-469ᵛ.
[89]Beauharnois to Minister, Sept. 24, 1742, *Ibid.*, C¹¹A, 77:108-112ᵛ. See also Memoir on Indians, Jan., 1743, *Ibid.*, C¹¹A, 80:361ᵛ-362; Minister to Beauharnois, Versailles, Mar. 24, 1744, *Ibid.*, B, 78:20ᵛ-21.
[90]The story of the migration of the Shawnee and its relation to the power of the French in the western country is given in detail in the author's "Shawneetown—A Chapter in the Indian History of Illinois," *Journal of the Illinois State Historical Society*, XXXII, no. 2 (June, 1939), pp. 193-205.
[91]The Memoir on Louisiana in 1746 estimates the strength of the Miami as three hundred warriors. *Arch. Nat., Col.*, C¹³A, 30:269. Johnson's estimation in 1763 gives the Miami as having 230, the Kickapoo, 180, the Mascoutin, 90, the Piankeshaw, 100, and the Wea, 200 fighting men. Pouchot, *op. cit.*, II, 260.
[92]In 1740 the French had trouble with the Pottawattomie at River St. Joseph when a Canadian killed one of their chiefs, Corbeau. Coulon de Villiers, the commandant, got them to go down to the governor to be conciliated, after all had been done that was possible to appease the chief's family at the post. See expense account, *Arch. Nat., Col.*, C¹¹A, 73:256, dated Apr. 15, 1740, showing 210 livres in goods used to "cover" the chief's death. Beauharnois to Minister, Quebec, Oct. 2, 1740 (*Ibid.*, C¹¹A, 74:13-14), says that 300 livres were spent. Forty livres were also spent in buying a slave to replace Corbeau (July 15, 1740), *Ibid.*, C¹¹A, 74:142. In October, 1741, a Wea named White Skin killed a Miami who was returning from the English. La Pérade kept the peace by promising the Miami to deliver the murderer. *Ibid.*, C¹¹A, 76:211-212.
[93]See account of the conference, July 8-28, 1742, in *Wisc. Hist. Coll.*, XVII, 380 ff. Also Beauharnois to Minister, Quebec, Aug. 14, 1742, *Arch. Nat., Col.*, C¹¹A, 77:83-84. The expense accounts show that these tribes were very active against the Chickasaw in these years.

Scattered about the region south of Lake Erie were roving bands of Seneca, Iroquois, and others, who presented a very special problem to the French. Though belonging to the Six Nations, these people seemed likely at times to cooperate with the French. This seemed the more possible with the outbreak of war in 1740 between the Seneca and the southern Indians, a movement much against the wishes of the English. The French had also enticed the Onondaga to enter this war, and it was they who in that year had destroyed a large Cherokee peace delegation which was being sent to them under English influence.[94] A famine among the Seneca in 1741 drove some of them to Canada for assistance, and this increased French influence with that tribe.[95] In the following year, they agreed to restrain their young men from raids on French commerce at the Niagara portage.[96] At the same time the French were also assured that the Onondaga and Seneca would not oppose them in the event of an English war.[97] Vagabond Seneca in the west pledged themselves to the French at Detroit and other places.[98] In the early part of the war, the English seem to have feared that Chartier contemplated leading a general attack of Shawnee and others against the Virginians and their Indian allies in the south—rumor having it that he was to invade that region with 500 men.[99]

But the French were soon aware that their hold on the nations to the south of Lake Erie was not secure unless they could control their trade. Thus we find De Noyan attempting to open up the trade there according to the governor's orders. In 1740 he sought a trader to send to the Great Miami River, but none would attempt it at his own expense. Finally the Sieur Laguin undertook to do so on the promise of the government to furnish goods for his own use and for Indian presents, he to equip himself and his *engagés*. The following spring he returned bringing some chiefs with him who submitted to French protection.[100] Laguin returned to that region in 1741 and drove out some English traders and a smith they had established there. Then De Noyan was recalled, and interest in the project lagged somewhat.[101] However, traders continued to go to this region, with the result that other Indians came there. In 1742, Céloron permitted some domiciliated Indians from Detroit to trade there, and he estimated the returns of their exploitation at some 200 packets of furs. Sieur Navarre, later sub-delegate of the intendant at Detroit, made an investigation of this trade, and his report was so favorable that

---
[94]Minister to Beauharnois, May 2, 1740, *Ibid.*, B, 70:342-342ᵛ.
[95]The Seneca to Beauharnois, Aug. 7, 1741, *Ibid.*, C¹¹A, 75:94.
[96]Minister to Beauharnois, Versailles, Apr. 20, 1742, *Ibid.*, B, 74:468-469ᵛ.
[97]Beauharnois to Minister, Quebec, Sept. 24, 1742, *Ibid.*, C¹¹A, 77:108-112ᵛ.
[98]*Ibid.*, C¹¹A, 79:179-180. Joined to a letter of the governor to minister, Oct. 13, 1743.
[99]John Ellis to Henry Morris, May 10, 1745, *Cal. of Va. State Papers*, I, 239.
[100]Scandal rose at Detroit against De Noyan over this matter. It seems he had first treated with one Simon Réaume, but later favored Laguin for the place. Doubtless De Noyan helped equip Laguin and shared in his profits. That seems to have been Réaume's criticism.
[101]De Noyan to Minister, Detroit, Aug. 20, 1742, *Arch. Nat., Col.*, C¹¹A, 78:348-354ᵛ.

the governor ordered two canoes to be sent there annually. These canoes were to be equipped at government expense and the proceeds were to go to the king. It was estimated that each canoe would earn a profit of 400 livres annually.[102]

Such was the status of affairs in that section just before the conspiracy of the western Indians against the French. That movement brought the Miami chief, *La Demoiselle*, to the front as the leader of these tribes. He welcomed English traders and soon built up a serious opposition to the French power in that region. De Bertet blamed him as the instigator of the threatened revolt in the Illinois in 1747, and actually planned a campaign into that section to destroy English influence.[103] Céloron's expedition into the Ohio was to be the answer of the governor to *La Demoiselle*.

At this point it becomes necessary to consider the war with the English and the part played by the west in that contest. Both sides expected a struggle on the lakes in the event of war, and, in 1741, the English are known to have considered building armed boats for use against those of the French. Such a force would make attacks on Forts Niagara and Frontenac more feasible.[104] This plan also included an attack on Louisbourg by sea. When Beauharnois heard of this plan he asked for artillery to arm the French barks, and even planned the immediate destruction of Oswego.[105] In 1742 he met the nations at Montreal and encouraged them in their wars with the Chickasaw, also cautioning them against the English.[106] In the meantime, French intrigue was active both north and south. Working through the Choctaw and the Spanish, they all but succeeded in turning the Creek against the English in Georgia, though Oglethorpe was finally able to hold his own against this peril, and to drive the Spanish invaders off the St. John's River. He reported the French influence as being very strong with the Catawba and Creek, and it was even believed that they were directing the Chickasaw and

---

[102]Hocquart and Beauharnois to Minister, Quebec, Oct. 10, 1743, *Ibid.*, C¹¹A, 79:44-46; Navarre's report, *Ibid.*, 48-49ᵛ, is joined to the above letter. An interpreter serving Navarre found at least ten nations in this region, including Seneca, Onondaga, Mohawk, Delaware, Abenaki, and Sauteur. There were about 500 to 600 men altogether according to this report, and the number was fast increasing. They welcomed the French traders, but did not wish to abandon the English, having learned that competition meant lower prices. The merchants at Detroit were said to oppose French trade in this region, charging that it damaged their trade. In 1744, two *congés* at 500 livres each were issued for the trade on the "River Blanche." Beauharnois and Hocquart to Minister, Quebec, Oct. 14, 1744, *Ibid.*, C¹¹A, 81:39-40ᵛ.
[103]Vaudreuil to Minister, New Orleans, Apr. 8, 1747, *Ibid.*, C¹³A, 31:54-54ᵛ. In 1749 an English trader was captured on the Wabash and sent to France, and there were rumors of an attempted English settlement in those parts. Vaudreuil to Minister, Sept. 22, 1749, *Ibid.*, C¹³A, 33:88ᵛ. Same to same, New Orleans, Aug. 26, 1749, *Ibid.*, C¹³A, 33:58-58ᵛ. This rumor may have grown out of the news of the organization of the Ohio Land Company, though this is doubtful. See *infra*, p. 96.
[104]The French had two brigantines on Lake Ontario, though one was wrecked at about this time. This plan seems to have been advanced by Lieut. Gov. Clarke of New York. See Clarke to Newcastle, Apr. 22, 1741, *Doc. Rel. to the Col. Hist. of N. Y.*, VI, 182-184. Clarke later detailed his scheme, which included the sending of a land force as well. He estimated 800 men were needed to build the vessels at some harbor on the lake and to protect the works. Clarke to Newcastle, June, 1743, *Ibid.*, 227 ff.
[105]Beauharnois to Minister, Quebec, Oct. 24, 1742, *Arch. Nat., Col.*, C¹¹A, 77:113-134ᵛ.
[106]See account in *Wisc. Hist. Coll.*, XVII, 380-409.

Cherokee as well.[107] In New York, rumor had it that the French, through their control of the Onondaga and Seneca, were ready to destroy Oswego, and it was said they could have accomplished this at that time without opposition from the Iroquois.[108]

When the war broke out with the English in 1744, Beauharnois planned to take the offensive at once. He hoped to organize the western Indians into two groups for two campaigns—the one to operate against the English in the Ohio valley and farther to the east, and the other to move toward the north and attack the Hudson Bay posts.[109] Accordingly, the Indians in the neighborhood of Michilimakinac and the post at Temiscamingue were to be assembled for an attack on the Hudson Bay posts in the following spring. The Indians of the neighborhood of La Vérendrye's posts were also to take part in this campaign, which, however, did not materialize.[110]

As for the attack planned upon the English on the Ohio, it fared little better. The Indians at Detroit and the Wea post were encouraged to take up the hatchet along with some from the Miami. This resulted in a considerable party being fitted out, consisting mostly of Ottawa. The party went into the Ohio country, but accomplished little or nothing, such an operation being too far from the base of supplies.[111] In fact, the English officer at Oswego reported at the end of the year that it was not known that any French Indians had gone against the English.[112] Beauharnois himself wrote next year that lack of supplies had hindered the execution of his plan and had forced him to abandon all thought of offensive action for the time being.[113]

By the spring of 1746, considerable supplies had been received,[114] and the governor was able to resume the offensive. In 1745, he had counselled with over 600 representatives of savage nations, one hundred fifty of whom were of the Six Nations. He was highly pleased with the responses of these and looked forward to their help in the war.[115] That autumn, he

[107]Oglethorpe to Clarke, Frederica, Apr. 22, 1743, *Doc. Rel. to the Col. Hist. of N. Y.*, VI, 242-243.
[108]Rutherford to Colden, Albany, Mar ?, 1742/43, *Colden Papers, N. Y. Hist. Soc. Coll.*, 1919, III, 9.
[109]Beauharnois to Minister, Quebec, Oct. 8, 1744, *Arch. Nat., Col.*, C¹¹A, 81:144 ff.
[110]La Vérendrye, skillful as he was in diplomacy, was never able to secure the aid of his strong Indian allies (the Cree, Christineaux, Assiniboines, and Sioux) for such a hazardous undertaking.
[111]Beauharnois to Minister, Quebec, Nov. 7, 1744, *Ibid.*, C¹¹A, 81:126-128ᵛ.
[112]See "Information of the Officer at Oswego abt Indian affairs, Decʳ 1744." *Penn. Arch.*, first ser., I, 665. Here he says: "We have made it our business to find out whether the Ffrench Indians had taken up the Hatchett against us; all we can learn is that at a Meeting between the Ffrench and Indians, severall ffatt cattle were killed and presented the latter, The Ffrench dancing after the Method of the Indians with the Heads of Beasts in their Hands, saying, thus will we carry the Heads of the English. The Indians in their turns danced, but said, thus will we carry the Heads of the Fflattheads, which made the Ffrench look very down, as they undoubtedly hoped to have been Joyn'd." The reference to the "Fflattheads" means that the Indians preferred to fight the Chickasaw rather than the English.
[113]Beauharnois to Minister, June ?, 1745, *Col. de Doc.*, III, 228.
[114]Over 100,000 lbs. of powder, 2,000 muskets, and 80 pieces of small ordinance were sent, and more promised in the next convoy. Minister to Beauharnois and Hocquart, Mar. 2, 1746, *Can. Arch. Rep.*, 1905, I, 70.
[115]Beauharnois to Minister, Quebec, Oct. 28, 1745, *Doc. Rel. to the Col. Hist. of N. Y.*, X, 19-21. The English were plagued to see the Iroquois go to Canada.

sent a group of officers among the western nations to lead them down to Montreal in the spring of 1746 to undertake raids against the English.[116] The response to this call was very good, and large numbers came down.[117] The French plan of offensive was to harass the borders of New England and New York by Indian raids. Large forces were concentrated near Montreal, to be ready in case the English carried out their threat to invade Canada from the south as well as by water from Quebec. Louisbourg having fallen in 1745, the English seemed likely to be able to accomplish this. The French had no intentions of making an attack upon Oswego, because such a policy would have alienated the Iroquois and very probably have driven them to fight on the side of the English.[118]

It would be tedious to attempt to trace in detail the different movements and campaigns undertaken by the French and Indians against the enemy. We shall notice only the more important. In November, 1745, a force of about 600 French and savages burned and plundered Saratoga, New York, taking over a hundred prisoners, mostly noncombatants. This was the first stroke of any importance, though small raids, chiefly against the New England settlements, were very numerous. During the winter, St. Pierre and De la Corne[119] lay near Fort St. Frederic with over two hundred French and Indians, to protect that post from any surprise by the English. They were relieved in the summer by De Muy[120] with a force about 450 strong, consisting largely of western Indians. This force spent some time on Wood Creek, felling trees so as to prevent the enemy from using that stream to descend on Fort St. Frederic. In August, Rigaud de Vaudreuil collected over 700 men, 400 of whom were Canadian militia. After wandering about through the forests for some time, this force fell upon Brookfield, Massachusetts, destroying the place and taking some thirty prisoners. Orange, the real objective, was not even attacked.[121] These raids put the English on the defensive, but otherwise had no effect except to terrorize the border settlements.

In the meantime, the English had collected provincial levies for the attack upon Canada, but the winter of 1746-1747 saw their forces dwindle away by death and desertion, while promised help from England failed

---

[116]Beauharnois to Minister, Quebec, Nov. 4, 1745, *Ibid.*, X, 27.
[117]La Corne, the elder, led down 192 from Michilimakinac, River St. Joseph, and *La Baye*, 80 of whom were women and children. *Arch. Nat., Col.*, C^{11}A, 87:70. A study of expense accounts shows that 520 western Indians of the different nations took part in the activities of 1746.
[118]Beauharnois to Minister, Quebec, 1744, *Ibid.*, C^{11}A, 81:146-149. All the English forts in New York were said to have been poorly garrisoned, but the French did not take advantage of this if indeed they were aware of it. Rutherford to Colden, Colden Papers, *N. Y. Hist. Soc. Coll.*, 1919, III, 112. The king suggested that the Seneca might be prevailed upon to destroy the English post at Oswego at a later time. Minister to Beauharnois, Versailles, Apr. 26, 1745, *Arch. Nat., Col.*, B, 81:34-34^v. Nothing, however, came of this. See King to La Jonquière, Apr. 1, 1746, *Ibid.*, B, 83:29^v-30.
[119]Luc de la Corne, Sieur de St. Luc, (1711-?), must not be confused with La Corne Dubreuil. Rigaud de Vaudreuil was a brother of the Louisiana governor.
[120]Jacques Pierre Daneaux, Sieur de Muy (1695-1758).
[121]The chief source for the military movements given above is the Journal of Occurrences, 1745-1746, *Doc. Rel. to the Col. Hist. of N. Y.*, X, 32 ff.

to come. However, the English did succeed in arousing part of the Six Nations to take the offensive against the French. Sir William Johnson had worked on this project since the beginning of the war and had succeeded so far as to get the Mohawk to make raids on the French near Montreal in 1745. Beauharnois, in the spring of 1746, collected his Indians and declared war on the Mohawk and rebellious elements of the Iroquois about the Sault and the Lake of the Two Mountains who had been aiding the enemy.[122]

The rest of the Six Nations remained neutral, but the Mohawk made serious attacks upon the French in the summer of 1747, though the last raid in June of that year was broken up with loss. La Corne estimated thirty to forty persons had lost their lives as a result of these raids, not including the last one in which several more lives were lost. In this case, however, the raiders themselves were nearly all killed or taken.[123] This stinging defeat at the hands of the French dampened the spirits of the Mohawk. Johnson himself was forced to admit that he was losing his influence with them, and they soon returned to their war with the Catawba in spite of his efforts.[124] In 1747, M. de Rigaud gathered a force of over 1,000 men with which he intended to block the threatened English attack on Fort St. Frederic. Most of the Montreal troops took part in this campaign, as a consequence of which it was necessary to transfer three hundred Quebec militiamen to defend Montreal. The expedition, faced with the usual difficulties of maintaining discipline among numerous savage allies, accomplished nothing and returned to Canada in July.[125]

The heavy expenditures for these campaigns soon exhausted the resources of the Montreal stores, while those at Quebec were in a similar condition due to the expenditures in the Acadian region. The burden of supporting the Indian allies was becoming unbearable. By the close of the year 1746 the French would have been glad to rid themselves of this horde, which was drawing at least a third of the total issues from the Montreal stores.[126] A great part of the burden came from the fact that vagabond Indians now began to come to both Montreal and Quebec, at-

---

[122] Journal of Operations, Mar. 8, 1746, *Arch. Nat., Col.*, C¹¹A, 87:26. Johnson's alliance with the Mohawk was not popular. Weiser especially opposed it as being unpolitic in reference to the rest of the Iroquois Confederacy. Johnson insisted, however, that he could depend upon the support of all the Six Nations and said: "I will engage to bring 1,000 Indian Warriours into the field in six weeks time, provided, I have clothes, arms and amunition for them or forfeit 1,000 pounds." Johnson to Clinton, July 17, 1747, *Doc. Rel. to the Col. Hist. of N. Y.*, VI, 386-387. For Weiser's argument, see Weiser to Peters, June 21, 1747, *Penn. Arch.*, first ser., I, 751. He said: "As to the Treaty of Col. Johnson and Mr. Lydias, with the Mohawks, I dislike it, and the Six Nations are offended at the people of Albany because we pay their people with goods against the opinion of the Chief Counsel." See also Weiser to Peters, July 20, 1747, *Penn. Arch.*, first ser., I, 761-762.
[123] La Corne's report, Oct. 8, 1747, *Doc. Rel. to the Col. Hist. of N. Y.*, X, 81-83. See also La Galissonière to Minister, Quebec, Sept. 15, 1747, in *Col. de Doc.*, III, 392.
[124] Johnson to Clinton, Jan. 22, 1749/50, *Sir William Johnson Papers*, I, 261-262.
[125] Abstract of Operations, 1746-1747, *Doc. Rel. to the Col. Hist. of N. Y.*, X, 99 ff.
[126] See expense accounts, *Arch. Nat., Col.*, C¹¹A, 87:80-80ᵛ. These bills of issues from the Montreal storehouses are usually given in amounts only, the prices not being given for the individual articles.

tracted by the hope of getting rations. The authorities reported: *"Nous sommes surcharges de tous ces gens la."*[127]

In 1747, most of the Indians were encouraged to return home when St. Pierre's convoy went up to Michilimakinac.[128] At the same time La Corne was sent back to the west to recruit a new force for service in the following spring.[129] But, in spite of these new plans for offensive action, the minister ordered Canada to fall back to the defensive for the spring of 1748.[130] News of the general suspension of hostilities came in August,[131] and both sides settled down to preparations for the renewal of the conflict which they were sure was to come in the near future.

It is appropriate at this point to give some account of French relations with the several Indian nations of the south and to show how the war with the English reacted upon French power in Louisiana. In order to understand conditions in that area at the outbreak of the war, it will be necessary first to sketch certain background factors.

The chief southern tribes were the Creeks, the Catawba, the Cherokee, the Chickasaw, and the Choctaw. Of these, the Cherokee were most powerful, numbering some 6,000 warriors. They were located on the upper Tennessee and ranged into the Carolinas and Georgia to the east. This great nation was friendly with the English and was not so warlike as the Chickasaw or Choctaw. The Chickasaw were located in the Yazoo country and had once been very powerful. At this time, however, they were reduced to only 600 warriors and were fast dwindling under the attacks of the Choctaw as well as of northern Indians, whom, as we have seen, the French encouraged to make war upon the Chickasaw. To the south and east of the Chickasaw in the Alabama uplands and the gulf region were the Choctaw, who could muster 4,000 fighting men. This nation was much devoted to the French, who encouraged their traditional hatred for the Chickasaw. To the north and east of the Choctaw were various smaller nations, such as the Alabama, the Abeka, and the Talapoucha, estimated to have all together some 2,000 warriors. These nations were loosely attached to the French, although receptive to English

---

[127]A study of expense accounts shows that out of 104 issues made to Indians and others at Montreal from September 1 to December 1, 1746, 30 were made to western Indians. *Ibid.*, C^{11}A, 86:178 ff. These Indians returned to their homes in August of 1747. Over 1,200 drew rations during that month, but it is certain that many were rationed twice. La Corne's party of Sac, Pottawattomie, *Folles Avoines*, Miami, and Illinois, 130 in all, included 28 men, 31 women, and 21 children of these tribes. Each man was given a blanket, each chief a fine coat, and each child a blanket. There were also issued 400 lbs. of powder, 600 lbs. of lead, 146 pots of brandy, 300 lbs. of tobacco, and other articles. Food supplies included 3,000 lbs. of biscuit, 960 lbs. of bacon, 25 *minots* of peas, 26 *minots* of corn, etc. Hocquart in October, 1747, submitted a bill for 33,000 livres for expenses for these Indians, *Ibid.*, 303-304.
[128]For equipment of this convoy, see *Ibid.*, C^{11}A, 117:304^v-306^v.
[129]Expense accounts show that he went equipped for extensive negotiation. He carried nearly a hundred thousand beads of wampum and had five interpreters. La Corne Dubreuil and Bellestre were to assist him. *Ibid.*, C^{11}A, 117:176. *Ibid.*, 360 and 360^v-361, shows that this party actually visited the Miami and Detroit. The minister's order to resume the defensive evidently put an end to these plans to recruit a new force of savages in the west.
[130]La Galissonière to Minister, Quebec, Nov. 6, 1747, *Col. de Doc.*, III, 399-400. Minister to La Galissonière, Mar. 6, 1748, *Can. Arch. Dep.*, 1905, 1, 105.
[131]Journal of Occurrences, 1747-1748, *Doc. Rel. to the Col. Hist. of N. Y.*, X, 174 ff.

intrigue because of their proximity to the Cherokee. The Creeks, a considerable nation, lived in the Georgia area and were allied to the English. To the north, on the Virginia-Carolina border, were the Catawba, a dwindling nation much subject to attack from the Six Nations, their enemies to the north. The Catawba relied on the English for protection. At the mouth of the Arkansas River lived the Arkansas Indians, who were staunch allies of the French.[132]

As has been explained above, the French had allied themselves to the Choctaw, thus earning the hatred of the Chickasaw. In 1731 this tribe had given refuge to the Natchez, who after the massacre of 1729 were fleeing French revenge. Consequently, in 1736, Bienville had waged a campaign against the Chickasaw, which, however, resulted in the French being badly worsted. Failing afterward to destroy the Chickasaw through encouraging attacks upon them by their savage enemies, the French had finally resolved upon another military campaign, which it was hoped would finally crush the Chickasaw power. A joint expedition was to be undertaken by Canadian and Louisiana forces, these being assisted by a number of French regulars. These forces were assembled at Fort Prudhomme on the Mississippi late in 1739.[133] The lateness of the season, the ravages of disease among the troops, the great difficulties of the terrain, and the procrastination of Bienville, who was in command, doomed the expedition to failure, and Bienville was finally content to sign a doubtful truce with the enemy, whom he had hardly been able to contact.[134] In the face of criticism resulting from this fiasco, Bienville tendered his resignation from the governorship of the colony.[135]

The Chickasaw continued to give trouble during the next few years, raiding convoys on the Mississippi frequently, and often penetrating into the lower Ohio. Bienville contended that part of this trouble was due to the fact that the Canadian government had refused to stop northern raiding parties from going against the Chickasaw.[136] Later, however, being

---

[132] On numbers and location of the several southern tribes, see the Memoir on the State of the Colony of Louisiana in 1746, *Arch. Nat., Col.*, C¹³A, 30:259-260; Pouchot, *op. cit.*, II, 259 ff.; Memoir of De Richarville, 1739, *Arch. Nat., Col.*, C¹³A, 4:202-205; Governor James Glen to Lords of Trade, Feb., 1747, *Public Record Office, Col. Off.*, 5, v. 372, 113; James Adair, *History of the American Indians*, 227, 232.

[133] Beauharnois to Minister, Quebec, Sept. 22, 1738, *Arch. Nat., Col.*, C¹¹A, 69:96-97; Hocquart to Minister, Sept. 30, 1739, *Ibid.*, C¹¹A, 69:236-239.

[134] The best source for information on this campaign is the *Dumche Ms.*, a journal kept by one of the French regular officers, and now in possession of the Chicago Historical Society. Bienville's journal has been printed in *Quebec Archives Reports, 1922-23*, 166 ff. A journal kept by Céloron de Blainville, one of the Canadian officers, is also printed in *Ibid.*, 157 ff. Shorter accounts may be found in Le Mascrier's *Dumont*, vol. II, and in Le Page Du Pratz, vol. III. A full account of the campaign is given in the author's "The Chickasaw Threat to French Control of the Mississippi," *Chronicles of Oklahoma*, XVI, 4 (Dec., 1938), 468-474.

[135] Bienville to Minister, New Orleans, June 18, 1740, *Arch. Nat., Col.*, C¹³A, 25:112-113ᵛ. The campaign cost nearly 1,000,000 livres! Bienville's successor, the Marquis de Vaudreuil, did not arrive in Louisiana until May 10, 1743.

[136] See Bienville to Minister, April 30, 1741, *Ibid.*, C¹³A, 26, 81-87; same to same, Sept. 30, 1741, *Ibid.*, 97-106; Salmon to Minister, May 4, 1745, *Ibid.*, C¹³A, 25:159-164ᵛ. The Canadian governor of course refused to recognize Bienville's "peace."

hard pressed by their enemies north and south, the Chickasaw did show signs of desiring peace.[137]

Bienville's failure against the Chickasaw dealt a serious blow to French prestige in Louisiana. Undoubtedly it was in part responsible for the defection of the Choctaw, which we shall note below, and its influence was noticeable as far away as the Illinois country, where Father Mercier reported that the news of the failure of the campaign had "strangely indisposed" the Illinois Indians against the French.[138] Some of these Indians were already interested in trading with the English on the Ohio, and one chief showed a noticeable sympathy for the Chickasaw.[139] The discovery of two canoes of Virginians on the Mississippi in the spring of 1742 caused the French to grow more uneasy in this regard.[140] Steps were actually taken in the Illinois country to prepare against a revolt in 1742, but nothing came of the matter.[141]

The result of the threatened revolt in the Illinois country was to force Bienville to prosecute the war on the Chickasaw with more vigor. Such heavy blows were dealt this tribe by Choctaw raiding parties in 1742 and 1743 that Bienville upon his retirement from office could report the Chickasaw power as being virtually broken.[142]

At this juncture the French suddenly found themselves faced with a revolt among the Choctaw. This movement was due to the most part to the scarcity of goods at the French posts resulting from the war with the English. However, the loss of French prestige as a result of the Chickasaw campaigns is also important. Then, too, one faction of the Choctaw had been trading with the English for several years. This faction, composed chiefly of the more remote towns, was led by the chief Red Shoe and his brother Mingo, who had established connections with James Adair, the noted English trader among the Chickasaw and Cherokee. Adair succeeded in making an alliance with Red Shoe and his followers, while Vaudreuil was finally forced to ask the loyal Choctaw to make war on the rebels. The French were somewhat strengthened in 1745 by the arrival of adequate supplies of merchandise and so sent an embassy to the rebel towns demanding Red Shoe's head. Though the embassy failed in this accomplishment, the French by withholding supplies from all the

---

[137]Bienville to Minister, Sept. 30, 1741, *Ibid.*, C¹³A, 26:97-106.
[138]Father Mercier to ———, Tamoroa Mission, May 27, 1741, *Ibid.*, C¹¹A, 75:214-214ᵛ.
[139]*Ibid.*, C¹³A, 27:85-86ᵛ.
[140]Bienville to Minister, New Orleans, July 30, 1742, *Ibid.*, C¹³A, 27:83-84. These men were Virginians, who seem to have been "exploring" the rivers. See the journal of John Peter Salling, a German who was with the party, in *Louisiana Historical Quarterly*, V, 3, 323-332. (The original is in the *Public Record Office*, Col. Off., 5, v. 1327, W65). See also the petition of John Heyward, leader of the party, asking the English king to procure their release, in *Ibid.*, 321-322. These men were kept in prison at New Orleans for some years, and all eventually returned to English hands through escape or capture.
[141]Beauharnois to Minister, Oct. 12, 1742, *Arch. Nat., Col.*, C¹¹E, 16:257-265ᵛ.
[142]Bienville to Minister, New Orleans, Feb. 18, 1742, *Ibid.*, C¹³A, 27:38-42ᵛ; same to same, Feb. 4, 1743, *Ibid.*, C¹³A, 28:31ᵛ-32ᵛ. The Chickasaw indeed sought peace with the French after 1743, but the outbreak of the war with the English prevented anything being accomplished. Except for minor raids, such as that on the Arkansas post in 1749, the Chickasaw gave no further trouble in this period.

towns succeeded in arousing the opinion of the majority against Red Shoe's faction.

In the meantime James Glen, the new English governor at Charleston, had become aware of conditions and had seized upon this opportunity to break the French hold on the Choctaw, which, if accomplished, might well have resulted in the loss of Louisiana to the French. Though Glen succeeded in securing considerable help from the legislature, he bungled the negotiations which he conducted with the Cherokee and the Creek, and by failing to secure the cooperation of Adair and other traders, he also lost their support, this being serious in itself. A new trading company, founded by Glen and his friends, failed to supply the rebellious Choctaw with the supplies they needed and so hastened the collapse of the rebellion. At the same time Glen lost the respect of the Cherokee and the Creek, his failure with the latter being largely due to his quarrel with the Georgia authorities over the distribution of the Indian presents. This quarrel was complicated by the fact that Mary Bosomworth, an alleged Creek princess, went into opposition to the English, taking with her a considerable element of the Creek nation. In the end the French not only succeeded in forcing the loyal Choctaw to deliver Red Shoe's head, but also practically exterminated the rebels.[143]

The net result of the course of events during this period, as far as Louisiana was concerned, was beneficial to the French. They had at last practically destroyed the Chickasaw and had proved themselves able to put down a first class rebellion among the Choctaw. English prestige among the southern tribes suffered accordingly. In spite of Adair's contentions, it is evident that the English were not yet able to supply the interior tribes with merchandise, and hence could not expect to exert political control over them. Throughout the remainder of the French regime, the French power in the lower Mississippi valley was to remain practically unquestioned.

---

[143]The story of the Choctaw rebellion and related problems during this period is discussed in detail in the author's "The Southern Frontier During King George's War," *Journal of Southern History*, VII, No. 1 (Feb., 1941), 37-54.

CHAPTER V

THE INDIAN UPRISING OF 1747 AND THE OHIO QUESTION

THE ENGLISH WAR caused the French to realize the danger of losing control over the Indians of the western country in both a political and an economic sense. Just as English penetration among the Cherokee and Chickasaw had by this time reached proportions which threatened French hegemony in the south, so also did penetration of traders from Pennsylvania and Virginia into the Ohio valley and the Great Lakes region bring home to the French in these parts the fear of losing their control over the western nations. The unrest of the Huron about Detroit and of the Ottawa at Michilimakinac in the earlier years of the decade under consideration is merely a prelude to this later trouble.

As soon as war broke out with the English, there resulted a great irregularity in the supply of merchandise for the western trade, partly because of unusual consumptions for war purposes,[1] and also because of interference on the part of English warships with French shipping. The English traders, on the other hand, were assured of more regular supplies, and were thus in a more favorable position to offer the savages the goods needed, much to the discomfiture of the French.

In 1745, M. de Longueuil wrote from Detroit that English traders were bargaining with the Indians about his post, telling them that the French would soon be driven from Canada, and that the English alone could be depended upon to supply the Indian trade. Longueuil says: "This news has had such a great effect in the villages of this post that they are constantly leaving without saying a word."[2] This was also reflected in the falling off of the interest of the savages in the war with the Chickasaw.[3] At the same time, Beauharnois had thought it advisable to guard against any possible attack on the trading convoy as it went up to the posts. Rumors of an Anglo-Indian attack on the convoy as it passed the Niagara portage were bruited about at that time. Though the western Indians sought to reassure the French, the governor remained cautious.

---
[1]From the usual channels of commerce, the government bought over 100,000 livres worth of goods as soon as the news of the declaration of war had reached the colony. This immediately caused a shortage of goods among the Montreal merchants. See Hocquart to Minister, Quebec, Oct. 29, 1744, *Arch. Nat., Col.*, C¹¹A, 82:159-159ᵛ.
[2]Longueuil to Beauharnois, July 28, 1745, *Ibid.*, C¹¹A, 83:61. A study of the expense accounts of the western posts reveals that an unusual shortage of goods had existed in the west since 1740. It was in this year that the troops returning from the Chickasaw campaign were rationed at the western posts for the return to the east. Michilimakinac, being out of the way was not affected, however. As we have seen above, some relief came in the years 1740-1743 when goods became more plentiful. Nevertheless, consumptions remained heavy during the years 1741-1743 on account of outlays to Indians going against the Chickasaw. Then followed the war with the English which continued to aggravate the evil.
[3]*Doc. Rel. to the Col. Hist. of N. Y.*, X, 19-21.

Conditions in the west did not improve during the year 1746. Goods continued scarce among the French, and the English continued their intrigues among the savages, working chiefly through the Six Nations.[4] In the early spring of the following year the French uncovered a well laid plot at Detroit in which it had been planned to make a surprise attack on the garrisons of the several posts. Fortunately a Huron woman had overheard the conspirators and carried the news to the missionary. The date of the outbreak had been set for one of the feasts of Pentecost. Longueuil immediately gathered all the people within the fort and made preparations for the defense of the place, with the meager force of only twenty-eight soldiers and the inhabitants. An additional handicap was found in the fact that supplies at the fort were low because this was the season just before the arrival of the spring convoy.

Longueuil suspected the English of being the source of the trouble, but it was difficult at the time to determine this, or even to learn what tribes were implicated in the conspiracy. At different times he conferred cautiously with the chiefs, and eventually concluded that the Huron were chiefly to blame, though even among this tribe there was a large loyal element led by the two chiefs—Sastaredzy and Taychatin. The Ottawa and Pottawattomie seemed at first to be loyal, or at least they led the French to think so. It was suspected that the renegade Huron, Nicolas, who had removed from Detroit to Sandusky, was the chief fomenter of the trouble. To divide the loyal from the disloyal, Longueuil insisted that those who kept their allegiance should go down to Montreal to get their presents according to custom, so that they might explain themselves to the governor, and so demonstrate their loyalty.

News of Indian raids accompanied by the burning of buildings and the slaughter of livestock now came in from the countryside about Detroit. The apprehension of the French at Detroit was increased by reports of the progress of the revolt at Sandusky, where five Frenchmen had been killed, and also at Michilimakinac where the Indians had risen. Then, too, the situation at Detroit grew worse with the spread of the rebellion among the Pottawattomie and the Ottawa, it being learned that these tribes had agreed to take possession of an island nearby which would enable the savages to control the eastern water passage to the post.[5] Widespread plots were uncovered in July, involving nearly all the tribes about Detroit in the conspiracy. The discovery of the scope of the conspiracy led the French to suspect that even the Chickasaw might have had

---

[4] Beauharnois to Minister, Oct. 15, 1745, *Arch. Nat., Col.,* C¹¹A, 83:99ᵛ-100ᵛ. The governor ordered Longueuil at this time to raise an Indian force to assist in the defense of Niagara if necessary. For information on the scarcity of goods in the west and its relation to the trouble, see La Galissonière to Minister, Oct. 22, 1747, *Ibid.,* C¹¹A, 87:260-261.
[5] The island was called *Isle aux Bois Blancs.* The chief sources for the study of the revolt are the "Memoir of Canada of 1747," by De Berthelot, *Arch. Nat., Col.,* C¹¹A, 87:16-21, and the "Journal of Occurrences of 1746-1747," in *Ibid.,* 22 ff. See also *Doc. Rel. to the Col. Hist. of N. Y.,* vol. X, pp. 83 ff.

a hand in it. No man dared leave the fort to go any distance away, and no crops were planted at Detroit that year.

In the meantime, Sieur Bellestre,[6] accompanied by the loyal chiefs, had made his way to Montreal, arriving there in July. He had with him several Detroit Ottawa, four Huron, including Sastaredzy and Taychatin, and a few other Indians. This group with a few others from other posts of the west made up the total of western Indians who came down to pay their respects to the governor that year. The general went into conference with them, seeking by diplomatic means to discover their grievances and to apply remedies. One of the requests made by the Huron was that the Jesuit, La Richardie, be returned to the Detroit mission, this being, as they said, one of the steps most necessary toward the restoration of order there. The general was obliged to comply with this, despite his dislike for the Jesuit.

While soothing the chiefs as well as he could, Beauharnois also gave orders for measures to be taken at the posts to stem the uprising. Bellestre was ordered to take over the command at River St. Joseph, and to serve as assistant to the Detroit commandant. M. de Longueuil was instructed to use his own judgment as to what course to follow in dealing with the revolt, except that he was to hold a firm course in demanding that those Indians who had murdered Frenchmen be surrendered for punishment, and that other rebels should prove their loyalty by turning against the English and bringing in scalps. The trading convoy was sent off for the west, after a long delay, guarded by a force of about one hundred men under Sieur Dubuisson.[7]

While the convoy experienced no difficulty in going up to the posts, French policy was weakened at this time by the outbreak of sickness among the loyal Indians who were returning with the convoy. Sastaredzy and Taychatin, head chiefs of the loyal element of the Huron, died. The loss of these two chieftains not only removed two of the most loyal friends of the French at Detroit, but it led the French to fear that the Huron rebels might suspect that foul play had resulted. Then, too, the departure of La Richardie was long delayed, poor health preventing his going up to Detroit that year.

When Dubuisson's convoy reached Detroit, Longueuil was reassured. He immediately took steps to answer calls for help from the Illinois and other nearby posts. Bellestre with twelve men was sent to River St.

---

[6]Marie François Picoté, Sieur de Bellestre (1719-?), spent most of his life at Detroit. He surrendered the place to the English in 1760. Bellestre had gone to the west with La Corne during the winter to recruit warriors for service at Montreal. *Arch. Nat., Col.,* C¹¹A, 87:75-77. He reached Montreal July 24, 1747.
[7]Dubuisson, whose full name does not appear, held various commands in the west, 1719-1748. In 1760 he was wounded at Quebec. For the equipment of this convoy, see expense accounts, *Arch. Nat., Col.,* C¹¹A, 117:279-281ᵛ, 308-309ᵛ. The force guarding the convoy consisted of eighty militia and a score of Abenaki, Iroquois, and Nepissing savages. Every effort was made to send up adequate supplies. The equipment for La Richardie's canoes was almost lavish, and his return to Detroit is certainly a striking contrast to his recall in 1742.

Joseph to take over the command there; La Pérade[8] with a small force was sent to the Wea post; and a few troops were sent to the Illinois in answer to De Bertet's plea for help.

Despite the fact that Longueuil was re-enforced at Detroit, he was still faced with an alarming shortage of provisions. The reasons for this are to be found in the fact that no crops were raised there in 1747, while the additional men sent up with the convoy, though bringing some food supplies, necessarily increased consumption. Then, too, the loyal elements of the Huron and Ottawa remained at the fort for rations, while the French dared not let them know how indigent they really were. Also new outbreaks occurred shortly, a series of attacks leading to the death of a settler at the hands of some Sauteur, who were reported to have sent the scalp to the English. At the Wea post, several Frenchmen were seized and held by the Miami as hostages. This was done at the instigation of the chief of the Sandusky Huron, Nicolas, who was fearful that some of the revolting savages were trying to treat with the French. It was reported that English traders at Sandusky were furnishing arms and ammunition for the support of the rebellion, and that these people were considering the establishment of a settlement there.

A second convoy was despatched under the command of St. Pierre, who was to take over the command at Michilimakinac; these canoes carried substantial re-enforcements in lead, powder, and other supplies.[9] The situation at Detroit now became more settled. A show of force on the part of the French, and the arrival of considerable goods for the trade had had a salutory effect.[10] That autumn, Nicolas and two other Huron chiefs began to make offers of peace, and deputies were sent to Longueuil.

While Longueuil was treating with these savages, wild rumors arrived telling of a raid against the French at La Grosse Isle near Detroit, it being first reported that three Frenchmen were slain. The deputies of Nicolas evidently knew the identity of the evil-doers. Fearing for their own safety, they told the French where the five men who had made the stroke were to be found, and a force sent out after them easily took four of them, and slew the fifth. These four—a Huron, a Seneca, and two Mohawk were put into irons. Although reports soon came that none of the French who had been attacked had been killed, Longueuil was now in position to bargain effectively with the rebels. The Huron, because they had revealed the identity of the outlaws, had drawn upon their heads

---
[8]Charles François Xavier Tarieu, Sieur de la Pérade, de la Naudière (1710-1775).
[9]See expense accounts in *Arch. Nat., Col.*, C¹¹A, 117:286 ff. Ten thousand beads of wampum and 640 pots of rum and brandy were sent for use in conferences. Supplies of lead and powder sent were less generous, Detroit getting only 1,800 lbs. of powder.
[10]The effect of the rebellion on the volume of trade has been discussed under the subject of the fur trade. What furs were collected at Detroit had to be held there for some time for fear of their loss in transit to Montreal.

the wrath of their confederates, and the tribe was obliged to intrench itself for protection against an anticipated attack. An open attack against the French was likewise rumored.

However, nothing came of these threats, and Ottawa and Sauteur from Michilimakinac and Saginaw soon came to ask pardon for those of their people who had killed Frenchmen. Early in January, the Huron from Sandusky also sent a deputation asking for the release of the prisoners held at Detroit. Acting upon the advice of the French and Indians at the post, Longueuil acquiesced and released the captives, though he seems to have had no definite promises from the rebels, particularly those at Detroit.[11] For this act, he was later censured by the government, since the policy of exemplar punishment for the rebels had been advocated. That this move was the politic one, however, was shown when in the following April, a general conference of Ottawa, Pottawattomie, Huron, and Sauteur was held at Detroit, at which all these tribes returned to French allegiance. When the convoy came up that summer with abundant supplies, the revolt was definitely over. That same year the tribes about Detroit went down in full force to meet the governor.[12]

Michilimakinac, as we have seen, had also experienced the rebellion. Here the Ottawa, Sauteur, and Mississague were affected. In 1747, three Frenchmen were killed while on their way from Detroit to Michilimakinac, and two canoes going to the posts of La Vérendrye were attacked near the entrance to Lake Michigan, one being lost with the crew of eight. Another man was stabbed in the vicinity of the post itself. All these things occurred in the absence of La Corne, the commandant, who had just gone down to Montreal with a band of western Indians who were to serve in the campaigns against New England and New York. St. Pierre was sent to Michilimakinac to take over La Corne's command, and De Verchères, the new commandant at *La Baye*, was ordered to assist him. No trading was to be attempted at the latter post until conditions became settled.

Disturbances also occurred at the more distant posts. A *voyageur* was robbed of his goods near Kamanistiquia, but no life was lost. Though conditions on the whole remained unsettled, some of the trading canoes continued to go out as before. Among the chiefs who worked for peace was the Ottawa, Pendalouan, who had done so much to influence his people to settle at *L'Arbre Croche*. He went down to visit Beauharnois in 1747, and did much to restore good relations between his people and

---

[11]Only three of the five were alive. As mentioned one had been killed when they were taken, and a second, the Seneca, had committed suicide when apprehended in an attempt to break jail. The others were released. The capture of these rebels, however, did nothing to intimidate Nicolas, "who always acts insolent and who has retired with some vagrants and English, where they are making threats." Madame Bégon to her son, Nov. 14, 1748, *Quebec Arch. Rep.*, 1934-35, 5.

[12]Longueuil's policy of conciliation was undoubtedly wiser than the policy of revenge advocated by Quebec officials far removed from the site of the trouble.

the French. When St. Pierre arrived at Michilimakinac with a large force and plentiful supplies, the trouble soon disappeared.[13] This convoy reached its destination in forty-five days, without mishap, and in view of the general peaceful conditions prevailing there the traders were sent out at once, although the governor had advised holding them at the fort so as to force the savages to come to the French to trade. This was a part of the governor's policy of bringing the Indians to surrender the members who had been guilty of murdering Frenchmen in the revolt. La Galissonière, the new governor, was especially committed toward a policy of punishment.

In the spring of 1748 the savages about Michilimakinac sent deputies to Montreal as usual, eighteen canoes setting out. They surrendered to the governor one of the rebels who had murdered a Frenchman, and this man was immediately placed in chains. This action was not pleasing to the savages who had not expected such harsh treatment. Nevertheless, they were forced to give up a second man whom the French had discovered as being one of those guilty of the attack on the canoes near the entrance of Lake Michigan. A few days later, the Indians from *La Baye* surrendered a third man.

The governor now seemed likely to succeed in his policy of chastisement, but an unfortunate accident changed affairs completely. As the three prisoners were being removed from Montreal to Quebec, they escaped by killing the soldiers who were conducting them.[14] The governor, greatly incensed, vainly tried to apprehend the fugitives as well as to discover those who must have assisted them to escape. The savages never formally atoned for their rebellion, and, though the governor still insisted that they must be brought to account, the post officers and traders seemed content from past experience to accept the restoration of peace as it was.[15]

It seems difficult to unravel the train of events in the Miami country at this time. The killing of the five French traders near Sandusky in 1747 was charged to Nicolas and his Huron village, but proof of this is

---

[13]Large supplies of food were sent with this convoy, including 9,600 lbs. of flour, 150 *minots* of corn, 70 *minots* of peas, 480 pots of brandy, and 160 pots of wine. There were also 30,000 beads of wampum sent for purposes of negotiating with the Indians. *Arch. Nat., Col.,* C¹¹A, 117:304ᵛ ff.

[14]This happened on Lake St. Pierre, just below Three Rivers. The three prisoners were doubtless aided by confederates from the shore. Being held in chains was considered by the savages as worse than death at the stake. The Detroit Indians were also represented in these conferences, the convoy of that year (1748) having created a very favorable impression as it went up under command of Céloron with over one hundred Frenchmen and Indians as guards. The number of *voyageurs* was also impressive. La Galissonière to Minister, Quebec, Oct. 23, 1748, *Doc. Rel. to the Col. Hist. of N. Y.,* X, 182.

[15]The western Indians, who had gone down to Montreal with La Corne just before the outbreak of the rebellion, do not seem to have been tainted with the revolt. Though they returned in large numbers in 1747, this was with French approval. The policy of punishing the Indians severely for insults to the French was extolled by some as most fitting. De Verchères at *La Baye* killed some Sauteur in 1748 for insults they gave, an act which Madame Bégon thought most proper. "If one had always chastised these nations, they would not be so insolent." Madame Bégon to her son, June 10, 1749, *Quebec Arch. Rep.,* 1934-1935, 73.

lacking.[16] Since no garrisons were ordinarily kept in that region, the sending of small forces there had the effect of restoring order and preventing further outbreaks. The Wea and Pottawattomie seemed to be generally loyal to the French, except at the Miami post where bad conditions existed.

In this vicinity was located the notorious Miami chief, *La Demoiselle*, whose relations with the English became known about this time, and whose insolence increased as the years went by. It was soon rumored that this chief had offered rewards for the scalps of both Douville, the commandant at the Miami post, and Longueuil at Detroit.[17] The Miami fort had been partly burned in 1747, and Dubuisson, who was sent there by Longueuil in the summer of that year, was able to do little more than to hold his position without attempting to repair the place, or to punish the murderers of a sixth Frenchman killed during the winter. Dubuisson negotiated with *La Demoiselle*, who was holding captive certain Frenchmen. In 1748 it was reported that the chief had returned to French allegiance. This seemed more likely because in that year plentiful supplies of merchandise were sent there. As we shall see, however, *La Demoiselle* really remained an enemy of the French.

As for Nicolas, he remained hostile and was said to have received the scalp of the Frenchman killed near the Miami in 1747. During the same winter he was reported to have been twice visited by Pennsylvania traders. Shortly thereafter he led his people away from the Sandusky locality and went either to *La Demoiselle's* village or to some place in the upper Ohio. The exact location of this tribe after 1748 is a mystery.

In the Illinois, though there was no actual revolt, rumors circulated to the effect that such a move was planned. As early as 1745, De Bertet had complained that the Illinois, though drawing out liberal amounts of powder and lead and other supplies for use against the Chickasaw, had been bringing in practically no scalps.[18] This report led Vaudreuil to threaten to punish these Indians unless they gave a better account of themselves.[19] Early in 1747 the French became aware of the fact that strange Indians were visiting the Illinois, proposing an alliance with the English. De Bertet, upon discovering these movements, immediately prepared for possible trouble.[20] Fort Chartres was in very bad repair, while the magazines there contained only a few hundred pounds of powder.

---

[16]Weiser gives us this idea of the identity of the guilty ones: "The Five French Indian Traders that were killed on the South side of Lake Erie, have been killed by some of the Six Nations (there called Acquanushioony, the name which . . . . signifys a Confederate)." *Penn. Col. Rec.*, V, 86-87.
[17]*La Demoiselle's* village, Pickawillany, was located on the Great Miami near the modern Piqua, Ohio.
[18]Vaudreuil to Minister, New Orleans, Oct. 30, 1745, *Arch. Nat., Col.*, C¹³A, 29:90-91ᵛ; Minister to Vaudreuil, Versailles, Apr. 30, 1745, *Ibid.*, B, 83:16.
[19]Vaudreuil to Minister, Mar. 15, 1747, *Ibid.*, C¹³A, 31:21ᵛ-22.
[20]See Journal of Occurrences, 1747-48, *Doc. Rel. to the Col. Hist. of N. Y.*, X, 142 ff.; Vaudreuil to Minister, March 22, 1747, *Arch. Nat., Col.*, C¹³A, 31:42-45, etc. It was at this time that the Illinois and Shawnee fell out.

Supplies of merchandise were likewise low, there being not a single ell of cloth in the stores. It had been fifteen months since De Bertet had received supplies from New Orleans, while trade with Canada was shut off.[21] Under these circumstances, it seemed advisable to collect the soldiers and inhabitants at Kaskaskia, to abandon the outlying settlements, and to call on Detroit and New Orleans for help. The situation seemed all the more serious because it was feared that the southern Indians were involved in this plot with the Illinois.[22]

Relief came in the autumn with the arrival of the convoy and the troops Longueuil had sent from Detroit. Nevertheless, the Illinois and Piankeshaw did attack the Shawnee, this being one of the reasons for the removal of the latter from the lower Ohio where they had located in 1745.[23] The following spring, De Bertet sent the chiefs who were suspected of being implicated in the conspiracy to New Orleans, where the governor interviewed them. Vaudreuil concluded that De Bertet's suspicions were largely unfounded, and the chiefs were sent back home exonerated.[24] However, roots of the conspiracy were still to be found in the Illinois as late as 1750, especially in relation to *La Demoiselle* and his machinations on the Miami. In that year the Kaskaskia and Cahokia were said to have received a belt from that direction. Rumor had it that *La Demoiselle* and his allies were to attack the French in the Illinois, and that the Missouri, the Osage, and the Sioux were to join in this enterprise.[25]

Such is the story of the Indian uprising in the west. Besides causing the French great losses in trade, and weakening their power at a time when all available strength was needed against the English, it had also occasioned great expense.[26] More important still was the loss of prestige which the French suffered with the western tribes. To recover this lost prestige, some thought harsh measures must be applied to the late rebels. The minister was one who advocated this policy in the extreme.[27] But such a course was not practicable. Canada, weakened as she was by the war, was content that the rebellion had been broken up, while the situation in the Ohio country was also demanding attention. In Louisiana, Vau-

---

[21]No congés were issued from Canada for the Illinois trade in these years.
[22]De Bertet to Sieur Lachine, trader at the Wea post, Oct. 20, 1747, *Doc. Rel. to the Col. Hist. of N. Y.*, X, 152.
[23]Vaudreuil to Minister, May 24, 1748, *Arch. Nat., Col.*, C¹³A, 32:64ᵛ-65.
[24]Vaudreuil to Minister, May 24, 1748, *Ibid.*, C¹³A, 32:63-64. The minister was also of the opinion that the end of the war with the English would remove all causes for further worry in the Illinois. Minister to Vaudreuil, Fontainebleau, Nov. 4, 1748, *Ibid.*, B, 87:15.
[25]Benoist de St. Clair to De Raymond, Ft. Chartres, Feb. 11, 1750, *Wisc. Hist. Coll.*, XVIII, 58-60. These fears were partially founded on the fact that the Sioux had recently murdered three Frenchmen on the upper Mississippi, while the Missouri had also killed a trader and his slave.
[26]In 1746-1747, over 75,000 livres were expended for this account. *Arch. Nat., Col.*, C¹¹A, 117:91-93, 144-146. See chapter on political and financial administration, above.
[27]Minister to La Jonquière, Marly, May 4, 1749, *Ibid.*, B, 89:66ᵛ-67; Minister to La Galissonière, Versailles, Feb. 12, 1748, *Wisc. Hist. Coll.*, XVII, 11. The minister once ordered Vaudreuil to send troops to the Illinois to chastise the rebels. Minister to Vaudreuil, Versailles, Nov. 4, 1748, in *Arch. Nat., Col.*, B, 87:13.

dreuil was busy enough with the Chickasaw, who at this time had just raided the Arkansas post.[28]

How far were the English to blame for the rebellion of the western tribes against the French? Naturally the French blamed the whole movement to English machinations with the savages,[29] but it would be difficult to prove that the English really knew what was going on at the time. As for their actually organizing the rebellion, it is certain that this was not done officially.[30] Of course, Croghan saw the opportunity of assisting the movement, and thought that if it were "purshued by some Small Presents," the French power about the Great Lakes could be destroyed.[31] Weiser, working on the same hypothesis, sounded out the Indians of western Pennsylvania as well as some few Indians from the Lake Erie country, and reported that he had learned much could be done toward driving the French out.[32]

It is to be observed that in both these cases, the English were acting after the rebellion had already started. They sought only to aid the movement, and with what success may be judged from the fact that Weiser was able to secure only two hundred pounds in goods from the Pennsylvania council to carry out this policy.[33] In New York, Clinton says he was aware of the movement in 1747, and that he had assurance of Indian aid if he would send a force to the west, but the trouble he was having with the assembly precluded his taking any action.[34]

In November, 1747, some of the Ohio Indians came to Philadelphia for a council meeting, and complained that they had "only little Sticks & Hickeries, and such things that will do little or no service against the hard Heads of the French."[35] Though the legislature voted a large present for these Indians, Weiser advised against sending it, saying that only a few Indians about Lake Erie were really opposing the French.[36] The following July, some of the western Indians, chiefly Miami, came to Lancaster to treat with the English. It was at this council that these Indians seem to have been admitted into official English friendship for the first time. Even then only eighteen western Indians were present.[37]

---

[28]This stroke was made in May, 1749, by Chickasaw and some Choctaw, six Frenchmen being killed, and eight women and children taken. Vaudreuil to Minister, Sept. 22, 1749, *Ibid.*, C¹³A, 33:83-86ᵛ. Even the Illinois convoy was in danger. Prisoners from this raid were surrendered to Gov. Glen of South Carolina.
[29]De Raymond to Minister, Nov. 2, 1747, *Ibid.*, C¹¹A, 89:225-226. La Galissonière to Minister, Oct. 22, 1747, *Ibid.*, C¹¹A, 87:260ᵛ-261; Longueuil to Beauharnois, July 28, 1745, *Ibid.*, C¹¹A, 83:61; De Berthelot's Memoir, *Ibid.*, C¹¹A, 87:16.
[30]*Penn. Arch.*, first ser., I, 741-742. The proposition is here made that the French be attacked in the west, it being assured that success would follow.
[31]Croghan to Peters, May 26, 1747, *Ibid.*, I, 742.
[32]Extracts from Weiser's letters, in Council Minutes, July 9, 1747, *Penn. Col. Rec.*, V, 84-86.
[33]Minutes of the Provincial Council, Sept. 25, 1747, *Ibid.*, 119-120.
[34]Clinton to Bedford, New York, Oct. 20, 1748, *Doc. Rel. to the Col. Hist. of N. Y.*, VI, 455.
[35]The council first voted 150 pounds, and later about 800 pounds. The Virginia legislature added 200 pounds to this amount. *Penn. Col. Rec.*, V, 146-147, 150-151. Weiser took the first present up in 1747, at which time he recommended sending a larger one. This last present ultimately was made in merchandise, including among other things, 18 barrels of powder, 20 hundredweight of lead, and 40 guns. *Ibid.*, 194-198, 257-258.
[36]Weiser to Peters, March 28, 1748, *Ibid.*, V, 212-213.
[37]For details of the council, see *Ibid.*, 299-300, 307-319. Also Weiser to Peters, Aug. 4, 1748, *Penn. Arch.*, first ser., II, 11-12.

After the council at Lancaster, Weiser set out for the Ohio to deliver the presents voted the fall before, and to investigate conditions in that region. He had special instructions to look into the situation among the Shawnee.[38] His trip into the forks of the Ohio did no more than to carry to the savages the news of the peace which had been signed in Europe, and to blaze new routes for trade with the western nations.[39]

So we conclude that English official aid to the revolt in the west came too late and in too small amounts to play any important part in the movement. The part played by private traders and rangers can only be surmised.

Inevitably, the cessation of hostilities in the west caused both sides to turn their eyes toward a future contest; for the peace of 1748 re-established the *status quo ante bellum* in the new world. In anticipating another struggle, the French in the west had good reason to study the lessons of the recent Indian revolt and the English threat by way of the Ohio. The French took a special interest in the Miami region, which was fast becoming a hot-bed of English intrigue. We have seen that De Bertet attributed the Illinois disturbance of 1747 to the machinations of *La Demoiselle*,[40] and many Frenchmen now began to consider the dangerous situation in the Ohio region as the result of shortsightedness in French policy. They called attention to the negligence and laxity which for years had allowed the English to encroach upon the French trade regions about the lakes. This had begun with the building of Oswego, which once tolerated, had continually grown as a menace to the French in the west; and, now, the English power had all but reached the Mississippi in its westward push.

De Raymond[41] was one of the chief proponents of the policy of destroying the English influence in the Ohio. In 1745 he had ventured to present a memoir upon the dangers of tolerating the English traders in the Miami region. From this center he saw their poison tainting the savages about the French posts to the north and west. It was the English who had fomented the revolt of 1747, one of the opening strokes of which had been the killing of the French traders at Sandusky. De Raymond pointed out that had the growth of English influence been nipped in the bud, such occurrences had been impossible.[42]

Nevertheless, he thought much could be done to alleviate the situation

---

[38]*Penn. Col. Rec.*, V, 290-293.
[39]*Ibid.*, 348-358. Weiser's journal kept on this occasion is also printed in Thwaites, *Early Western Travels*, I, 21-44.
[40]Journal of Occurrences, 1747-1748, *Doc. Rel. to the Col. Hist. of N. Y.*, X, 142-143.
[41]De Raymond, in command at the Miami post, and attentive to the drift of things in that region, gives one of the best analyses of the whole Ohio question from the French point of view.
[42]De Raymond to Minister, Nov. 2, 1747, *Arch. Nat., Col.*, C11A, 89:225-228. Pouchot, writing with the benefit of experiences of the war in which France lost her colonies, was of the opinion that had she fortified the Miami region instead of the upper Ohio, she had been better off. His argument was that fortifications in the Miami region would have been effective in stopping English influence with the western Indians, while at the same time the English would not have been incensed at such action on the part of the French.

by securing a favorable peace at the close of the war then in progress. Such a peace to his way of thinking would provide (1) that the English should give up Oswego and forever renounce their claim to the Iroquois nations, (2) that they should renounce all claims of trading rights in the Ohio valley, and (3) that all English traders in that region should forthwith retire. What a contrast this was to the actual peace! No wonder this zealous officer wrote a year later: *"Plus de chemain pour aller au detroit, miamis, ouyatanons, illinois et misisipy."*[43]

La Galissonière shared this feeling, though he felt it less intensely than the officer who had had direct contact with the problem. Nevertheless, by 1748, he had determined upon a policy of opposing the English on the Ohio and its tributaries by force, peace or no peace. It should be mentioned, incidentally, that the French had not yet suspected the English designs of colonizing on the Ohio as exemplified in the founding of the "Ohio Company" among the Virginians.[44]

The English continued their policy of subsidizing the Indians who came to Oswego, with ammunition and supplies, encouraging them to continue to trade there and to oppose the French governor in his anti-English

---

[43]De Raymond to Minister, Sept. 8, 1748, *Arch. Nat., Col.*, C11A, 92:338v.
[44]Journal of Occurrences, 1747-48, *Doc. Rel. to the Col. Hist. of N. Y.*, X, 179. Here La Galissonière said: "Though we be at peace, every attempt of the English to settle at River à la Roche, White river, the Beautiful River, or any of their tributaries, must be resisted by force...." See also Margry, VI, 665. The writer seems to have in mind here only trading posts, not agricultural settlements. In spite of the possible interpretation which may be put on this quotation to the contrary, I am not convinced that the French were at this time actually aware of the plan of the Virginians to found a new settlement west of the Alleghenies. The founding of the Ohio Company goes back to Nov. 3, 1747, when Lieut. Gov. Gooch first mentions an application for transmontane grants. The Lords of Trade wondered why the Virginians had asked for royal permission to make land grants. "We desire you will acquaint us, as soon as possible, what Difficulties you are under with Respect to making such Grants as you mention." Lords of Trade to Gooch, Whitehall, Jan. 13, 1747/8, *Virginia Correspondence*, 408-409, *Pub. Rec. Off., Col. Off.*, 5, v. 1366. The Lords referred Gooch's letter to Newcastle, and also to the Privy Council and the king. Lords to Newcastle, 1748, same date. In the meantime Gooch had replied (June 16, 1748), explaining that "these Lands lie upon some of the chief Branches of the Mississippi" and expressing the fear that "such Grant might possibly give some Umbrage to the French, especially when we were in hopes of entring into a Treaty establishing a General Peace." Quoted in Lords of Trade to Privy Council, Sept. 2, 1748, *Ibid.*, 411-412. This same source reveals the request of the Virginians for a grant of 200,000 acres, they to be given four years in which to survey the land and construct a fort for defense. The Lords approved the request, suggesting that "all due Encouragement ought to be given to the extending [sic] the British settlements beyond the Great Mountains." Their only qualm was to be found in the fact that people already settled in Virginia might be anxious to move out, leaving His Majesty's quit rents unpaid. *Ibid.*, 414-416. On Nov. 24, 1748, the Privy Council gave its approval to the scheme, ordering that no person already settled in Virginia was to remove westward unless he continued to pay quit rents in Virginia. Gooch was also instructed to make sure that the associates built a fort and provided for adequate protection for the settlers. Lords to Privy Council, Whitehall, Dec. 13, 1748, *Virginia Corr.*, 422-425, *Pub. Rec. Off., Col. Off.*, 5, v. 1366. The grant itself was made on Feb. 23, 1748/9 under orders of the council dated Feb. 9, in favor of John Hawley, Thomas Lee, Thomas Nelson, Col. Cresap, Col. Wm. Thornton, Wm. Nimmo, Daniel Cresap, John Carlisle, Lawrence and Augustus Washington, Geo. Fairfax, Jacob Gyles, Nathaniel Chapman, and James Woodrop. The first three were English merchants or councilmen, the others Virginians. They were granted 500,000 acres "betwixt Romanettos & Buffaloes Creek on the South side of the River Alligane otherwise the Ohio and betwixt the two Creeks and the Yellow Creek on the North side of the River," though another site might be chosen if desirable. The associates were to receive 200,000 acres immediately, provided they agreed to send one hundred families west of the mountains within seven years. The land was granted free of quit rents for ten years, provided the company gave adequate protection to the settlers. As soon as this first grant was settled, the other 300,000 acres were to be granted. Lords to Privy Council, Whitehall, Feb. 23, 1748/9. *Virginia Corr., Ibid.*, 427-433; Lords to Gooch, same date, *Ibid.*, 434-439. The home government thus took a step calculated as "a proper Step towards checking the Encroachment of the French by interrupting part of their Communication from their Lodgements upon the great Lakes to the River Mississippi." Such an action was tantamount to renewing war with the French, who, however, were not yet aware of this. Lords to Gooch, Mar. 4, 1748/9, *Ibid.*, 439-443. Céloron, in making his trip into the Ohio, was looking for English traders, not land speculators.

policy.⁴⁵ That the English were not so confident of their success, however, is shown by Johnson's statement at this time, which gives a pessimistic outlook upon the ability of the English to turn the Indians against the French.⁴⁶ The French on their part decided to find out what the status of affairs in the Ohio country really was, by seizing the opportunity to send a force there, which would serve the double purpose of warning the English to leave the country, and of demonstrating to the savages the intention of the French toward them.⁴⁷

Under the command of the veteran Céloron, a force of two hundred French and thirty savages set out for the Ohio in the middle of June. Having reached Niagara, they made the portage around the falls, ascended Chautauqua Creek, which debouches near the outlet of Lake Erie, and made the portage to the upper Allegheny. Near the present Warren, Pennsylvania, Céloron buried the first of the famous leaden plates which declared the Ohio and its tributaries to be French. Others were buried at different points as the expedition descended the rivers. At Logstown the French found the English flag flying and ordered it taken down. The savages here and at Scioto farther down showed considerable hostility, though they dared not attack so large a force. The French commander not only harangued the savages, but he also ordered the English traders whom he found to leave the region, at the same time sending by them similar messages of warning to their governments. Though the size of the French force did something to awe the savages, Céloron's diplomacy was weakened by the fact that he carried no merchandise for the trade or for presents. It is also plain that his promises in regard to the establishment of French traders in that region were none too specific. Having reached the mouth of the Great Miami, the French expedition began the ascent of that stream, thus leaving the Ohio. At the mouth of Laramie's Creek they found the village of *La Demoiselle* and spent some days in conferences with this chief, in the course of which they secured his formal promise to return to the Miami post the following spring along with his people. After burning the boats and surplus baggage, the expedition then made the portage, arriving at the Miami post a few days later. Early in October the expedition reached the Detroit River and, having secured supplies and boats, descended to Montreal, arriving at this place in the middle of the following month.⁴⁸

---

⁴⁵Clinton to Bedford, May 30, 1749, *Doc. Rel. to the Col. Hist. of N. Y.*, VI, 484-485.
⁴⁶Johnson in a letter to Peter Warren on July 24, 1749, says: "It is that Interest with ye Indians that makes, our Neighbours the French an over match as we have woefully known this War. The Wolfe never Values how many the Sheep are, and it is a very unequal war between us & them." *Sir Wm. Johnson Papers*, I, 239.
⁴⁷The plans for this expedition seem to have been well guarded. The authority for it is in Minister to La Galissonière, Versailles, Jan. 2, 1749, *Can. Arch. Rep.*, 1905, I, 110. The purpose of the expedition according to Madame Bégon was "to hunt the English who have established themselves among the Miami and to make there a French establishment . . . ." Madame Bégon to her son, June 13, 1749, *Quebec Arch. Rep.*, 1934-1935, 74.
⁴⁸The journal kept by Céloron on this expedition may be found in Margry, VI, 666 ff. For the journal kept by Father Bonnécamps, the Jesuit scientist who accompanied the expedition, see Thwaites, *Jes. Rel.*, 69, 150 ff. Space does not permit a detailed account of the expedition here. An excellent account may be found in Parkman.

The effects of this expedition were immediate and far-reaching. The French had finally ascertained the real temper of the Indians in the Ohio valley, and the great difficulties they were to encounter in overcoming the English power in that region. Céloron himself gives us some conclusions on these points at the close of his journal: "I do not know by what means they (he refers to the Ohio savages) could be led back. If one uses violence, they will take refuge in flight. They have a handy place of refuge among the Flat Heads, from whom they are not far removed. If one chooses to penetrate there by commercial enterprise, our traders can never deliver merchandise at the price at which the English sell it, this by reason of the great expenses they will be obliged to make . . . ." He thought, on the other hand, that if an attempt was made to subsidize the Ohio trade, it would work to the prejudice of the trade at the other posts in the west, and so be harmful in the long run. As to the idea of setting up new posts in the Ohio region, there was also the inconvenience of additional expense. Such was the situation as seen by Céloron, a veteran observer of conditions in the west.

To the English, the sending of the expedition into the Ohio came as a great surprise. Croghan, after having word of the departure of the French force, thought that the course to be followed was that along the south side of the lake to the Miami country. He discredited rumors that the French were to go down the Ohio, thinking this a false report put out by the Virginians to deceive the Pennsylvanians in regard to the activities of the former in the Ohio land schemes.[49] In New York, on the other hand, the opinion was that the French actually intended to chastise the Ohio Indians who had favored the English during the late war, as well as to cut off the English trade in that region.[50] As to the effect of Céloron's expedition upon the Indians of the Ohio valley, it is certain that it did more harm than good. It was claimed that these Indians were on the brink of attacking the French party as it advanced, as indeed is borne out by the journals of both Céloron and Bonnécamps.[51]

In any case, both French and English began to act to secure all possible advantages in the Ohio region. In January, 1750, Johnson wrote: "The French were never so active among the Indians as at present . . . ," while at the same time he said the English were hampered by lack of support from the government.[52] It was rumored that the French governor

---

[49]Croghan to ———, July 3, 1749, *Penn. Arch.*, first ser., II, 31. The formation of a land enterprise in the Ohio valley by the Virginians had caused a good deal of jealousy on the part of the Pennsylvanians. See Lee to Hamilton, Nov. 22, 1749, *Penn. Col. Rec.*, V, 422-423.
[50]Colden to Shirley, New York, July 25, 1749, *N. Y. Hist. Soc. Coll.*, 1920, IV, 126. The English also thought this a move on the part of the French to intimidate the Iroquois into signing a separate peace with them.
[51]The English traders of course paid no heed to Céloron's warnings that they cease to trade in the Ohio country. See Hamilton to Clinton, Philadelphia, Oct. 2, 1749, *Doc. Rel. to the Col. Hist. of N. Y.*, VI, 530-531. They felt secure in the protection of the savages with whom they traded.
[52]Johnson to Clinton, Jan. 6, 1750, in *Ibid.*, 546.

meant to return that spring with another force, possibly to attack and destroy the Six Nations.[53] This led Johnson to prepare these Indians for any such contingency by advising them "to keep their Warriors home least the French, who are a designing people, should surprise them . . . ." He also urged the governments of New York and Pennsylvania to "exert themselves so as to counterballance the Favors of the French."[54]

At the same time, La Jonquière presented a strong protest to the English upon the subject of their activities in the Ohio region, accompanying this with copies of messages sent by the English at Oswego to stir up the savages against the French. He also charged that these messages were accompanied with war belts, the calumet, and English flags.[55] La Galissonière, upon retiring from the governorship, drew up a long memoir on the state of the colony and its future, in which he advocated the immediate strengthening of the settlement about Crown Point, and the fortifying of Abbé Piquet's village on the St. Lawrence. He also condemned the existence of Oswego, and advised that twice as many troops be sent to the colony as were then there. He thought these measures would keep the English within their boundaries.[56]

In the Illinois, another threat of rebellion among the savages appeared in 1750, seemingly as a result of Céloron's expedition. This movement was attributed to Croghan, who was said to be working through *La Demoiselle* on a scheme to get the nations in that vicinity to join with those of the Illinois and Missouri to destroy the French. The promise of cheap goods to be supplied by the English traders was to be the reward for those who took part in the movement. The French connected the murder of one of their people at River St. Joseph at this time with this conspiracy.[57] Though the watchfulness of Benoist and De Raymond seems to have prevented the outbreak, the French daily grew more alarmed at the growth of *La Demoiselle's* village and the corresponding English influence in that section. It was soon evident that force was the only means left to remove this menace to the French power in the west.[58] This course was approved by the minister, but he was not in favor of building new fortifications in the Ohio valley, at least to any extent. He argued that the forts at Detroit and Niagara would, if well garrisoned, be enough to keep the lakes open, especially since the building of the new

---

[53] Johnson's meeting with the Mohawk, Feb. 2, 1749/50, in *Ibid.*, 548-549.
[54] Johnson to Clinton, Feb. 19, 1749/50, in *Ibid.*, 547. In this letter he gave an exaggerated estimate of the plentiful supply of presents which the French were sending out to the Indians of the Ohio country, and the great danger that existed that they would win back the nations while the close-fisted assembly refused to vote presents.
[55] La Jonquière to Phips, Quebec, Mar. 7, 1750, *Ibid.*, 565-566.
[56] *Ibid.*, X, 227-229.
[57] Benoist de St. Clair to Capt. De Raymond, Ft. Chartres, Feb. 11, 1750, *Wisc. Hist. Coll.*, XVIII, 58-62; Minister to Vaudreuil, Versailles, Sept. 26, 1750, *Arch. Nat., Col.*, B, 91:14; Minister to La Jonquière and Bigot, May 3, 1750, *Wisc. Hist. Coll.*, XVIII, 62.
[58] Michel to Minister, New Orleans, July 3, 1750, *Arch. Nat., Col.*, C¹³A, 34:321-323. The minister had already approved of La Jonquière's sending a force against *La Demoiselle* under date of Sept. 30, 1750. Minister to Vaudreuil, Versailles, *Ibid.*, B, 91:22.

post at Toronto.[59] Though the French hesitated for the moment to extend their line of fortifications into the Ohio valley, this course was the next to be taken. The next few years were to bring the armed forces of both rivals face to face in the disputed region.

[59]The post at Toronto was begun in 1749 with the purpose of intercepting trade that was going to Oswego by that route. La Jonquière's proposals of Sept. 20, 1749, were for the building of several commercial posts in the Ohio valley, with a fort near the headwaters of that river. La Jonquière to Minister, Quebec, Margry, VI, 727-728. The minister agreed to the establishment of one such post, but argued against an extensive system of works, on the ground that they would only serve to lengthen the frontier to be defended and thus further divide the forces of the colony. He also referred to the item of expenses involved in any large undertaking. See Minister to La Jonquière, May 19, 1750, *Can. Arch. Rep.*, 1905, I, 133. The argument of La Galissonière for such a post as well as his many reasons why the French should anticipate the English in such action are given in his memoir of 1750 in *Doc. Rel. to the Col. Hist. of N. Y.*, X, 229-230. See also Margry, VI, 665. La Galissonière blamed the English that the French had not already settled the Ohio valley, meaning that fear of their interference had kept out French settlers. In connection with the proposed building of the forts in the Ohio region, it should be mentioned that the French had considered for several years the building of a fort near the mouth of the Ohio. After the Shawnee moved to that region in 1745 new interest was taken in the matter, and the permission of the government to begin the project was obtained. However, no money was made available, and in 1746, the project was dropped. The Shawnee as we have seen soon left that area, and dreams of gathering a strong community of savages there came to naught. The fort on the lower Ohio was considered quite as much in regard to the Chickasaw menace as in regard to that of the English. The subject is discussed in detail in the author's "Shawneetown—A Chapter in the Indian History of Illinois," *Journal of the Illinois State Historical Society*, XXXII, 2 (June, 1939), 193-205.

SUMMARY AND CONCLUSIONS

THIS STUDY of the French regime in the Mississippi valley during the 1740's seems to warrant the following conclusions:

(1) Concerning the political administration, it would be almost trite to point out that the constitution of the Old Regime was utterly unfit for the conditions of frontier life. Just as John Locke's "Fundamental Constitutions" failed to thrive in the Carolinas, so also did the semi-feudal constitution of France fail in the Mississippi valley. The attempt to regulate the lives of frontiersmen and traders at Detroit or Michilimakinac from Marly or Versailles was of course doomed to failure. However, in justification of the colonial governments, it should be pointed out that they might conceivably have given a better account of themselves had colonial finances been put on a sound basis, and more especially had adequate funds been provided. We are impressed that throughout this period the annual administrative expenses of France's chief colonies hardly equalled in amount the yearly pensions of single Versailles courtiers. Paternalism, unfit as it was to cope with problems of the new world, might still have been more successful had it been better supported financially.

(2) The imperative necessity of strengthening the colonies of Canada and Louisiana came to be realized by all thinking Frenchmen in this period. When it is recalled that the single English colony of New York had at this time approximately twice the number of inhabitants found in Canada and Louisiana combined, the need is all the more evident. Though the government gave much verbal encouragement to the increase of population, and especially to the development of agriculture, practically nothing of a concrete nature was done to meet these problems. It was, therefore, evident that if France was to maintain her hold on her North American colonies, both in controlling the Indians and in opposing English expansion, a large emigration from the mother country or other European nations to these regions was a necessity. That the government in this period contented itself with sending over a few convicted salt smugglers and a handful of bureaucrats seems hardly intelligible, even after allowance has been made for the ban on non-Catholic immigration to New France.

(3) In regard to the fur trade, we conclude that the French, though hard pressed by English competition in the eastern area, were still able to supply the continental markets with beaver. Though the English had firmly established their trade in the lower lakes region and in the upper Ohio country, it must be remembered that these disadvantages were more than offset by the extension of the French trading area to the upper

Mississippi region and (under the La Vérendryes) into the far northwest. Even the difficulties met during the war and the Indian rebellion in the upper country did not fundamentally alter things in this regard. In fact, beavers were already rapidly diminishing in numbers in the eastern region. It has also been shown that the English traders in the south were not yet able to challenge seriously the French hold on the lower Mississippi tribes. On the other hand, it has been pointed out that men like La Galissonière foresaw the eventual decline of the fur trade in any case, and realized that agriculture must soon assume its rightful place as the basic occupation of New France.

(4) From our study of Indian affairs during this period we can only concede to the French their superiority in handling the savages. Considering the vast areas which they governed and the very great handicaps in supplying merchandise to the distant savages who had already become dependent upon the white man's goods, it is a wonder that the French managed as well as they did. The Indian rebellion in the upper country in 1747 and that of the Choctaw in the south can be largely attributed to the failure of the French to supply trade goods to the tribes, and not to any failure of French diplomacy. Under similar conditions the English might well have fared worse. We are assured that the French were ready to profit by the lessons drawn from these events.

(5) Finally, Frenchmen of this period realized fully the role of the colonies in the future struggle with England. The superiority of the English colonies in population and wealth was taken for granted. Despite great difficulties, France must strengthen her colonies, and particularly the western country, against the threatened English advance. In this struggle she could reasonably assume that she would be assisted by the bulk of the Indian nations of the interior. The fate of the French colonies was inextricably bound with that of the mother country in the great international struggle then at hand.

BIBLIOGRAPHY

MANUSCRIPT SOURCES

Archives Nationales, Colonies. The material in the French archives is by far the most important source for any study of this period. Transcripts and photostats of the pertinent documents are to be had in the Illinois Historical Survey at the University of Illinois, Urbana. The series used most extensively are B, comprising letters and documents sent out by the French central authorities to the colonial officials, C¹³A, containing correspondence from Louisiana officials to the home government, and C¹¹A, containing letters and despatches from Canada to the home government. Most of the material relating to Canada, chiefly in series A, B, C¹¹A, C¹¹E, and F, including the so-called Collection Moreau St. Méry, is found in calendar form in the *Canadian Archives Reports* for 1883, 1885, 1886, 1887, 1889, 1899 Supplement, 1904, and 1905 (Ottawa, 1884-1905). The material containing expense accounts for the western posts is found in the series C¹¹A, volumes 73-117.

Archives Nationales, Marine. Some reference has been made to series B⁴ of this material in the Paris archives, with special reference to the Chickasaw campaign in 1739-1740.

Chicago Historical Society, O. L. Schmidt Collection. The papers in the *Schmidt Collection* deal chiefly with business transactions and are valuable from that standpoint. There are also numerous manuscripts of a miscellaneous nature which are in the hands of the Society in addition to the *Schmidt Collection*. All those pertinent to this period have been consulted.

Newberry Library, Edward E. Ayer Collection. This great collection, consisting largely of miscellaneous private papers, has been found very valuable. The maps of this collection are excellent.

Public Record Office, Colonial Office, 5. The documents consulted are found chiefly in volumes 371, 372, 373, and 455, though scattered documents from other volumes have been used. A large part of this material consists of the records of the council and assembly of South Carolina which have never been published. Photostats in the Illinois Historical Survey.

Vaudreuil Manuscripts. This material, in the form of a letter book, consists of one hundred and forty-six letters and documents from the correspondence of the Marquis de Vaudreuil and his officers from 1743 to 1747. This material, a part of the *Louden Mss.*, is now in the Huntington Library; photostats in the Illinois Historical Survey.

PUBLISHED SOURCES

ADAIR, JAMES, *The History of the American Indians; particularly those Nations adjoining to the Mississippi, East and West Florida, Georgia, South and North Carolina, and Virginia, etc*, London, 1775.

Aulneau Collection, edited by the Rev. Arthur K. Jones, S. J., Montreal, Archives of St. Mary's College, 1893. This collection contains letters of Jesuit fathers to Madame Aulneau, mother of the Father Aulneau who was slain by the Sioux with La Vérendrye's son in 1736.

BACQUEVILLE DE LA POTHERIE, CLAUDE CHARLES LE ROY, *Voyage de L'Amérique, contenant ce qui s'est passé de plus remarquable dans l'Amérique septentrionale depuis 1534 jusqu' à présent,* 4 vols., Amsterdam, 1723. La Potherie gives one of the best and most detailed accounts of the Indian tribes about the Great Lakes.

BLAIR, EMMA HELEN, *The Indian Tribes of the Upper Mississippi Valley and Region of the Great Lakes,* Cleveland, 1911. Miss Blair has taken selections from Perrot, La Potherie, and others, and has translated them with notes.

BREESE, SIDNEY, *The Early History of Illinois, from its discovery by the French in 1673, until its cession to Great Britain in 1763, including the narrative of Marquette's discovery of the Mississippi,* Chicago, 1884. Though of very little value as a secondary account, the book has a long appendix containing some documents on Illinois under the French.

BURPEE, LAWRENCE J. (ed.), *Journals and Letters of Pierre Gaultier de Varennes de la Vérendrye and his sons, with correspondence between the governors of Canada and the French court, touching the search for the western sea,* Champlain Society Publications, vol. XVII, Toronto, 1927. This collection contains nearly all the material relative to this subject and is very well annotated.

Calendar of Virginia State Papers and Other Manuscripts, 11 vols., Richmond, 1875-1893. This is a very rich collection of letters and state documents for the Virginia commonwealth. Vol. I contains materials suitable for this period.

Canadian Archives. This great body of material is unfortunately poorly arranged. There are three series of publications which may be arranged under this head. First is the *Canadian Archives Reports,* 1883-1910, referred to above, and containing 29 volumes. A second series of publications is called *Public Archives of Canada,* 1912-1934, containing 14 volumes. Thirdly there is the *Publications of the Canadian Archives,* 1909-1930, also containing 14 volumes. All are published at Ottawa. As mentioned above, the first, or *Canadian Archives Reports,* contains chiefly calendars of archives materials. The others contain usually the documents transcribed.

CHARLEVOIX, PIERRE FRANÇOIS XAVIER DE, *Histoire et description générale de la Nouvelle France, avec le journal historique d'un voyage fait par ordre du roi dans l'Amérique Septentrionale,* 6 vols., Paris, 1744. This work is scholarly and contains very excellent maps and cuts of natural life.

COLDEN, CADWALLADER, *History of the Five Indian Nations of Canada, which are dependent on the province of New York, and are a barrier between the English and the French in that part of the world,* 2 vols., New York, 1904. Here Colden, as a member of the New York Provincial Council and as a student of Indians, discusses the Iroquois problem in relation to Franco-English affairs.

Collection de Manuscrits contenant Lettres, Mémoires, et autres Documents Historiques Relatifs à la Nouvelle France, 4 vols., 1883-1885, Quebec. This collection is taken from archives material at Quebec.

Collections of the Massachusetts Historical Society, 77 vols., Boston, 1792-1927. The wide correspondence of the Massachusetts governor in this period, William Shirley, serves as a background for the study at hand. This includes the arrangements for the Louisburg campaign in 1745 and the plans for other campaigns against Canada from New York in 1746 and 1747, and various other subjects in all of which the Massachusetts papers are very helpful. The volumes used in this study are nos. 6 and 7 in series VI and no. 1 in series I.

Collections of the State Historical Society of Wisconsin, 31 vols., Madison, 1854-1931. Under the direction and editorship of the late Reuben Gold Thwaites, this society published a very valuable collection of documents relative to the history of the Wisconsin region during the period of the domination of the French and later. Most of this material has been taken from the Paris archives. Vols. XVII and XVIII are pertinent to this period.

Colonial Records of Connecticut, 15 vols., Hartford, 1850-1890. Of chief value in this collection is the record of the colonial council.

Colonial Records of North Carolina, 12 vols., Raleigh, 1886-1895. This consists chiefly of the journal of the provincial assembly. It is rich in documents concerning the Indian situation in the south.

Correspondence of William Shirley, 1731-1760, edited by Charles H. Lincoln, 2 vols., New York, 1912. Though some serious omissions are found, this collection contains most of the works of Shirley with notes including the sources from which the different documents are taken.

Documents Relative to the Colonial History of the State of New York, edited by E. B. O'Callaghan, 15 vols., Albany, 1855-1887. This great collection, drawn from the archives of Paris and London, remains as the chief printed collection of this material. Vols. VI and X contain appropriate material for this period.

DUMONT, DIT MONTIGNY, JEAN BENJAMIN FRANÇOIS, *Mémoires Historiques sur la Louisiane*, 2 vols., Paris, 1753. This work is an abridgement by Le Mascrier of the *"Mémoire de L— D— officier Ingenieur Contenant Les Evénemens qui se sont passés à Louisiane depuis 1715 jusqu'à présent. Ainsi que ses remarques sur les moeurs, usages, et forces des diverses nations de l'Amérique Septentrionale et de ses productions,"* which is now in the Newberry Library. I have used both these works. Le Mascrier naturally censured the original Dumont very drastically in his edition. The publication of the *Dumont Ms.* would be a boon to scholars of this period. See Jean Delanglez, "A Louisiana Poet-Historian: Dumont dit Montigny," *Mid America*, XIX, No. 1 (January, 1937), pp. 31-49.

DUNN, CAROLINE and ELEANOR, "Indiana's First War," *Indiana Historical Society Publications*, vol. 8, no. 2, Indianapolis, 1924. This is a collection of documents taken from the *Archives Nationales* relative to the Chickasaw campaigns of 1736 and later.

Edits, Ordonnances Royaux, Declarations et Arrêts du Conseil d'Etat du Roi Concernant Canada, 3 vols., Quebec, 1855. This collection contains documents of both the French council of state relative to the regulation of Canadian affairs, and of the Canadian superior council. This includes the council records, *ordonnances* of the governors and intendants, and so on.

English Colonial Treaties with the American Indians, edited by H. F. Depuy, New York, 1917. This collection is composed of the chief treaties entered into by the northern colonies with the Indian tribes, including some facsimiles of title pages and the like.

Great Britain—House of Commons, ... Report from the committee appointed to inquire into the state & condition of the countries adjoining to Hudson's Bay & of the trade carried on there. London, 1749.

Historical Collections, Michigan Pioneer and Historical Society, 40 vols., Lansing, 1874-1929. Of especial use for the period under consideration are the local papers, such as the Cadillac collection at Detroit; printed in vols. 33 and 34.

HOUGH, F. B. (ed.), *Memoir upon the late war in North America between the French and the English, 1755-1760 ....*, by M. Pouchot, Chevalier of the Royal and Military Order of St. Louis; Former Captain of the Regiment of Béarn; Commandant of Forts Niagara and Lévis in Canada, 2 vols., Roxbury, Mass., 1866. This memoir is very valuable for information upon the Indians of Canada as well as upon the Canadian people themselves.

Indiana Historical Society Publications, 10 vols., 1897-1933, Indianapolis. Though this collection is not rich in sources on the whole, vol. 8 contains some good material on the Chickasaw wars, and vol. 3 has some valuable documents concerning the French mission on the Ouabache.

JOHNSON, SIR WILLIAM, *Papers*, 4 vols., Albany, 1921. Consists of the complete correspondence of the great New York Indian trader and agent.

KALM, PETER, *Travels into North America; containing its Natural History in General ....*, 3 vols., Warrington and London, 1770-1771. Kalm is very valuable for accounts of social, agricultural, and industrial conditions of the colonies, both French and English.

Le Page du Pratz, *Histoire de la Louisiane, contenant le découverte de ce vast pays; sa description geographique; un voyage dans les terres; l'histoire naturelle, les moeurs, coutumes & religion des naturels, avec leurs origines; deux voyages dans le nord du Nouveau Mexique, dont un jusqu'à la mer du sud . . . .*, 3 vols., Paris, 1758. Le Page's history is not so good, but his descriptions of Indian life, especially among the Natchez, are classic.

Louisiana Historical Collections, edited by B. F. French, 5 vols., New York, 1846-1853. This is a good collection but was not very extensive.

Louisiana Historical Quarterly, 20 vols., Baton Rouge, 1917-1937. These publications, consisting almost entirely of local archives material, are very valuable. The archives of the Cabildo at New Orleans have yielded the records of the Louisiana Superior Council as well as many other valuable papers. Nearly all these volumes contain pertinent material. Vols. III and IV contain the *Cabildo Archives* papers, while vols. X-XIX contain the records of the superior council.

Margry, Pierre, *Découvertes et Etablissements,* 6 vols., Paris, 1888. Margry still remains one of the best general collections. Vol. VI contains Céloron's Journal and some papers on La Vérendrye.

Massicotte, E.-Z., "Arrêts, Edits, Ordonnances, Mandements et Règlements Conservés dans les Archives du Palais de Justice de Montréal," *Trans. Roy. Soc. of Canada,* 3rd ser., vol. XI, pp. 147-174.

Mereness, Newton D. (ed.), *Travels in the American Colonies,* New York, 1916. A short collection of early travels, including the journals of Antoine Bonnefoy and Major de Beauchamp relative to the trouble with the Chickasaw and Choctaw.

Mitchell, John, *The Contest in America between Great Britain and France . . . .*, London, 1757. This work gives the British arguments in the Ohio valley controversy as well as in regard to other regions being disputed with the French.

New Jersey Archives, or Documents Relative to the Colonial History of New Jersey. Contains the journal of the provincial assembly as well as other documents, first ser., 35 vols., Newark and Trenton, 1880-1939. Certain volumes contain newspaper clippings from various colonial newspapers. Vol. XII is valuable for such material. Provincial council records for this period are found in vols. XV-XVI.

New York Evening Post, photostats in the Illinois Historical Survey, Urbana. The files are practically complete for the years 1744-1750.

New York Historical Society, Collections, 66 vols., New York, 1868-1933. Among the various other documents are found the Colden Papers (Vols. 50-56), consisting of the letters and papers of Cadwallader Colden and his correspondents, both in American affairs and in foreign relations.

Pennsylvania Archives, first ser., 12 vols., Philadelphia, 1853-1856. The collection consists almost entirely of the correspondence of Pennsylvania officials. It is the best arranged collection of this period. Vols. I and II were used.

Pennsylvania Colonial Records, 16 vols., Philadelphia, 1852. This collection contains the journal of the proceedings of the provincial council only, but it is rich in other material in the form of letters and depositions made to or before the council which were included in the record. Vols. IV and V are appropriate for this study.

Provincial Papers, Documents and Records Relating to the Province of New Hampshire, 33 vols., Nashua, 1867-1915. In the period under consideration, we find in this collection the voluminous correspondence of B. Wentworth, the provincial governor, which is printed in vol. V.

Rapport de l'Archiviste de la Province de Quebec, 1921-22 to 1932-36, 15 vols., Quebec. The series is edited by P. G. Roy. This material includes calendars of the notarial registers of Quebec, and also of the registers of *congés* issued for the western trade, besides many other documents found in the various archives of the city of Quebec, most of which are printed in full.

Recueils de Règlemens, Edits, Declarations et Arrêts, Concernant le Commerce, l'Administration de la Justice, & la Police des Colonies Françaises de l'Amérique, & les Engagés. Avec le Code Noir, etc., Paris, 1765.

Report from the Committee Appointed to Inquire into the States and Condition of the Countries Adjoining to Hudson's Bay, and of the Trade carried on there (1749). This report resulted from an investigation ordered by the House of Commons, concerning the activities of the Hudson's Bay Company and the general condition of trade in that region.

SHORTT, ADAM, *Documents Relative to Money, Exchange and Finances of Canada Under the French Regime*, 2 vols., Ottawa, 1926. This is a special publication under *Canadian Archives* and consists of selected documents from the Paris archives and the various Canadian repositories.

South Dakota Historical Collections, 17 vols., Pierre, 1902-1934. The material in this collection that is pertinent to the period under consideration consists of papers on the subject of La Vérendrye and his sons and their efforts at discovery in the northwest. This material is found in vol. VII.

THWAITES, REUBEN GOLD (ed.), *Early Western Travels, 1748-1846; a series of annotated reprints of some of the best and rarest contemporary volumes of travel, descriptive of the aborigines and social and economic conditions in the middle and far west, during the period of early American settlement*, 32 vols., Cleveland, 1904. The first volume of this collection contains the journal of Conrad Weiser on his journey to the Indians of the forks of the Ohio in 1748.

―――, *The Jesuit Relations and Allied Documents—Travels and explorations of the Jesuit missionaries in New France*, 1610-1701, 73 vols., Cleveland, 1904. This great collection, printed in France contemporaneously, is the greatest single collection of documents relative to the history of Canada and Louisiana excepting the governmental correspondence. Vols. 69 and 70 have been used.

WRAXALL, PETER, *An Abridgment of Indian affairs contained in four folio volumes, transacted in the colony of New York, from the year 1678 to the year 1751*, edited with an introduction and notes by Charles Howard McIlwain, Cambridge, 1915. This work summarizes Anglo-Indian relations in New York by giving in chronological order summaries of all conferences and diplomatic relations with the Indians in that region.

SECONDARY WORKS

Books

ALVORD, CLARENCE WALWORTH, *The Illinois Country, 1673-1818*, vol. I, *Centennial History of Illinois*, Springfield, 1920. This is by far the best work on the French regime in Illinois. The bibliography is elaborate.

BONNASSIEUX, PIERRE, *Les Grandes Compagnies de Commerce*, Paris, 1892. This is chiefly a historical sketch of the great European trading companies, and is necessarily brief because of its wide scope. It is, however, of very sound scholarship.

BURPEE, LAWRENCE JOHNSTONE, *The Search for the Western Sea*, London, 1908. Of the many works on the subject of La Vérendrye, this contains the best account.

CRANE, VERNER W., *The Southern Frontier, 1670-1732*, Philadelphia, 1929. This book, excellently done, emphasizes Anglo-French commercial rivalry in the south.

GAYARRÉ, CHARLES, *History of Louisiana*, 4 vols., New Orleans, F. F. Hansell and Bro., Ltd., 1903. This remains as the best work on general Louisiana history.

GIPSON, LAWRENCE HENRY, *Zones of International Friction: North America, South of the Great Lakes Region, 1748-1754*, New York, 1939.

HANNA, CHARLES A., *The Wilderness Trail, or The Ventures and Adventures of the Pennsylvania Traders on the Allegheny Path, etc.*, New York, G. P. Putnam's Sons, 1911. This is a very thorough work, rich in biography, place locations, and photographs, including a few maps.

HODGE, FREDERICK WEBB, *Handbook of American Indians North of Mexico*, 2 vols., Washington, Government Printing Office, 1910-1911. (Smithsonian Institution, Bureau of American Ethnology, Bulletin 30). This is the definitive work on this subject.

HOUCK, LOUIS, *A History of Missouri from the Earliest Explorations and Settlements until the Admission of the State into the Union*. 3 vols., Chicago, R. R. Donnelley and Sons Company, 1908. Though lacking in many respects, this work embodies a mass of material on early Missouri history.

HUGHES, THOMAS, S. J., *History of the Society of Jesus in North America, Colonial and Federal*, 2 vols., New York, Longmans, Green, and Co., 1917. Scholarly and thorough. It gives a good account, not only of administrative features, but also of social life of the Jesuits at the Indian missions.

INNIS, HAROLD A., *The Fur Trade in Canada—An Introduction to Canadian Economic History*, New Haven, Yale University Press, 1930. This is by far the best work on the subject, but in places is poorly organized. The author has not used the Paris archives materials except in printed or calendared form.

KELLOGG, LOUISE PHELPS, *The French Regime in Wisconsin and the Northwest*, published by the State Historical Society of Wisconsin, Madison, 1925. This work, done from printed sources only, has additional faults in that the author is sometimes careless.

MERIWETHER, ROBERT L., *The Expansion of South Carolina, 1729-1765*, Kingsport, Tennessee, 1940.

MUNRO, WILLIAM BENNETT, *The Seigniorial System in Canada; A Study in French Colonial Policy*, New York, Longmans, Green, and Co., 1907. This is the standard work on this subject.

PARKMAN, FRANCIS, *A Half Century of Conflict*, 2 vols., Boston, Little, Brown, and Company, 1906. Parkman weaves sound historical scholarship into a fascinating narrative. His faults were those of the men of his school and age in that they indulged in personal feelings.

————, *The Old Regime in Canada*, 2 vols., Boston, Little, Brown, and Company, 1910. Volume 2 remains one of the best works on the constitutional, financial, and administrative phases of the government.

QUAIFE, MILO MILTON, *Chicago and the Old Northwest*, 1673-1835. An excellent treatise on the Chicago portage section.

ROY, J.-EDMUND, *Histoire du Notariat au Canada*, 4 vols., Lévis Imprimé a *La Révue Du Notariat*, 1890.

SEVERANCE, FRANK H., *An Old Frontier of France; the Niagara region and adjacent lakes under French control*, 2 vols., New York, 1917. A good piece of work is marred by the author's carelessness, resulting in numerous errors and omissions.

SHEA, JOHN GILMARY, *The Catholic Church in Colonial Days, 1521-1763*, New York, 1866. This work is of considerable value for church history in the west. Shea has had access to most of the local church archives.

SULTE, BENJAMIN, *Histoire des Canadiens Français*, 8 vols. in 4, Montreal, 1882. Of value for identification of persons chiefly, though the historical survey it encloses is competent.

————, *Mélanges Historiques*, G. Ducharme libraire-editeur, Quebec and Montreal, 1918.

SURREY, Mrs. NANCY MILLER, *Calendar of Manuscripts in Paris Archives and Libraries relating to the history of the Mississippi valley to 1803*, Washington, 1926-1928.

————, *The Commerce of Louisiana during the French Regime, 1699-1763*, New York, 1916. Gives finest details and is fully authentic.

TANGUAY, CYPRIEN, *Dictionnaire Généalogique des Familles Canadiennes depuis la fondation de la colonie jusqu'à nos jours par l'abbé Cyprien Tanguay*, 7 vols., Quebec, 1871-1890.

VILLIERS DU TERRAGE, BARON MARC DE, *Les Dernières Années de la Louisiane Française*, Paris, 1903. Though dealing chiefly with the later period, the author has given a concise summary of the history of early Louisiana in the first chapter.
VOLWILER, ALBERT T., *George Croghan and the Westward Movement, 1741-1782*, Cleveland, 1926. In this able essay, the author attempts to defend the thesis that Croghan's work in relation to western development is more important than that of Boone.
WILLSON, HENRY BECKLES, *The Great Company (1667-1871), being a history of the honourable company of merchants—adventurers trading into Hudson's Bay*, London, 1900. This is a rather sketchy essay, undocumented for the most part. It serves as a background to English trading activities in the northwest.
WINSOR, JUSTIN, *The Mississippi Basin, The Struggles in America between England and France, 1697-1763*, Boston and New York, 1898. This book really opened up the field of western history. It remains as the definitive work on the subject. It is especially rich in contemporary maps which the author has reproduced in considerable numbers.
WRONG, GEORGE M., *The Rise and Fall of New France*, 2 vols., New York, 1928. Wrong gives in a scholarly manner an excellent short treatise on the subject. His work comes close to being that which fills a great need, the need for a modern history of the French colonies.

Monographs

ANDREWS, CHARLES M., "Anglo-French Commercial Rivalry, 1700-1750: The Western Phase," *American Historical Review*, XX, nos. 3 and 4 (April and July, 1915), pp. 539-556, 761-780. Andrews deals mostly with the international aspects of the subject, and he is not specific about the western trade.
BEUCKMAN, (REVEREND) FREDERICK, "Civil and Ecclesiastical Jurisdiction in Early Illinois," *Illinois Catholic Historical Review*, I, no. 1 (July, 1918), pp. 64-71. This work, being a sketchy account, is more historical than technical.
————, "The Commons of Kaskaskia, Cahokia and Prairie du Rocher," *Illinois Catholic Historical Review*, I, no. 4 (April, 1919), pp. 405-412. Essential facts are given here, as well as a map of the commons.
BUFFINGTON, ARTHUR H., "Albany Policy and Westward Expansion," *Mississippi Valley Historical Review*, VIII, no. 4 (March, 1922), pp. 327-366. This is an able discussion of the Anglo-French commercial rivalry about the lower Lakes Region, but it lacks documentation from French archives.
BURPEE, LAWRENCE J., "Highways of the Fur Trade," *Trans. of the Royal Society of Canada*, 3rd ser., vol. VIII, pp. 183-192.
CALDWELL, NORMAN W., "The Chickasaw Threat to French Control of the Mississippi in the 1740's," *Chronicles of Oklahoma*, XVI, no. 4 (December, 1938), pp. 465-492.
————, "Shawneetown—A Chapter in the Indian History of Illinois," *Journal of the Illinois State Historical Society*, XXXII, no. 2 (June, 1939), pp. 193-205.
————, "The Southern Frontier During King George's War," *The Journal of Southern History*, VII, no. 1 (February, 1941), pp. 37-54.
CARON, IVANHOE, ABBÉ DE, "Les Evèqués de Quebec, Leurs Procureurs et leurs vicaires generaux, à Rome, à Paris et à Londres (1734-1934)," *Trans. Roy. Soc. of Canada*, 3rd ser., vol. 29, sec. I, pp. 151-178.
DUNN, JACOB PIATT, "The Mission to the Ouabache," *Indiana Historical Society Publications*, vol. 3, no. 4 (1902), pp. 255-330. Dunn has written a scholarly account of the mission there, and he has also added an appendix which contains reprints of documents from the *Archives Nationales*, Paris.
FRANKLIN, W. NEIL, "Pennsylvania-Virginia Rivalry for the Indian Trade of the Ohio Valley," *Mississippi Valley Historical Review*, XX, no. 4 (March, 1934), pp. 463-480. This work deals adequately with the lack of cooperation between these two colonies in the face of French opposition.

JOHNSON, IDA AMANDA, "The Michigan Fur Trade," *Michigan Historical Publications,* University ser., vol. V (1919), pp. 1-201. This is a narrative written from printed sources, in which the writer neglects economic interpretation.

LOMASNEY, PATRICK J., "The Canadian Jesuits and the Fur Trade," *Mid-America, An Historical Review* (Formerly *Illinois Catholic Historical Review*), IV, no. 3 (January, 1933), pp. 139-150. Though this article shows some bias, it is scholarly.

MASSICOTTE, E.-Z., "Les tribunaux et les officiers de justice, à Montréal, sous le régime français, 1648-1760," *Trans. Roy. Soc. of Can.,* 3rd ser., X, 273-303. Gives a complete list of officers of justice and tribunals in the Montreal jurisdiction. Very valuable.

————, "Mémento Historique de Montréal 1636-1760," *Trans. Roy. Soc. of Canada,* 3rd ser., vol. XXVII, pp. 111-131. Lists all officials at Montreal in that time, even to church organists.

————, (ed.), "Un recensement inédit de Montréal, en 1741," *Trans. Roy. Soc. of Canada,* 3rd ser., vol. XV, sec. I, pp. 1-61.

MUNRO, WILLIAM B., "The Office of Intendant in New France: A Study of French Colonial Policy," *American Historical Review,* XII, no. 1 (October, 1906), pp. 15-38. This remains the best article on this subject.

RIDDELL, Hon. WILLIAM RENWICK, "Le Code Noir," *Trans. Roy. Soc. of Canada,* 3rd ser., vol. XIX, sec. II, pp. 33-38.

ROY, PIERRE-GEORGES, "Les Conseillers au Conseil Souverain de la Nouvelle France," *Trans. Roy. Soc. of Canada,* 3rd ser., IX, pp. 173-187.

SHIELS, W. EUGENE, "The Jesuits in Ohio in the Eighteenth Century," *Mid-America, An Historical Review,* VII, no. 1 (January, 1936), pp. 27-47. This contains a valuable account of the Sandusky settlement of Huron and La Richardie's activities there. The author had access only to printed sources.

THWAITES, REUBEN GOLD, "Notes on Early Lead Mining in the Fever (or Galena) River Region," *Wisconsin Historical Collections,* vol. XIII (1895), pp. 271-292. Inasmuch as this is not intended for a formal treatise on the subject, it is necessarily sketchy.

————, "The Story of Mackinac," *Wisconsin Historical Collections,* vol. XIV (1898), pp. 1-16. Thwaites gives a rather sketchy account of the development and importance of Michilimakinac, and the scholarship is not of the best.

WOOD, GEORGE A., "Céloron de Blainville and French Expansion in the Ohio Valley," *Mississippi Valley Historical Review,* IX, no. 4 (March, 1923), pp. 302-319. This is a scholarly monograph on the Ohio valley controversy, 1749-1752.

INDEX

Adair, James, 84, 85
Agriculture, 40ff.
 encouragement at Detroit, 43-44
 experiments with bison wool, 46
 flour production in Illinois, 41-42
 livestock, 45-46
 methods, 41
 mission tenure at Detroit, 44-45
 prices of grain, 45
Anguirot, Huron chief, 65
Augé, Etienne, 55, 56
Aumônier, office of, 15
"Bad Bread" Mutiny, 1745, 13
Beauharnois, Charles de la Buache, Marquis de, 10, 11, 13, 22, 33, 53, 54, 57, 58, 65, 66, 67, 68, 69, 70, 71, 72, 73, 74, 75, 76, 78, 79, 81, 86, 88, 90
Beauharnois, Claude de, 66, 67, 68
Bellestre, Marie François Picoté, Sieur de, 88
Bienville, Jean Baptiste le Moyne, Sieur de, 25, 73, 83, 84
Bigot, François, 44, 55
Black Code, 17
Bonnécamps, Father Joseph Pierre de, 44, 98
Bordereau, defined, 25
Bosomworth, Mary, 85
Cadillac, Antoine la Mothe, Sieur de, 44
Canada, administration, 11-12
 finances and revenues, 28ff.
 health of people, 39
 moral and religious conditions, 39-40
 population, 20, 36-37
 ratio of men to women, 37-38
 western posts and settlements, 37
Capuchins, 19
Céloron, Pierre Joseph, Sieur de Bienville, 32, 43, 44, 55, 68, 69, 70, 77, 78, 97, 98, 99
Chalet, François, 54
Champigny, Chevalier de, 23
Chartier, Peter, 76, 77
Chickasaw War, 23, 25, 26, 30, 34, 39, 60, 62, 65, 67, 76, 78, 83, 84, 86
Choctaw Rebellion, 1747, 84-85
Church and State, relations, 18ff.
 controversy over liquor traffic, 20ff.
 regulation of religious orders, 20
 subsidies for religious work, 19

Clinton, George, 94
Colden, Cadwallader, 51
Colonial Council, organization and duties, 15-16
Company of the Indies, 15, 25, 28, 47, 51, 58, 59
Convoy System, in Louisiana, 27-28
Coureurs de bois, abuses, 74
 deserters, 13
 moral problem, 39
 regulation, 55ff.
Coutume de Paris, 16
Croghan, George, 94, 98, 99
Dailleboust, 10
De Bertet, 40, 47, 75, 78, 89, 92, 93, 95
De Lorme, Pierre, 10
De Muy, Jacques Pierre Daneaux, Sieur, 80
De Léry, Chaussegros, 44
De Noyan, Pierre Jacques Payan, Sieur, 14, 37, 54, 66, 67, 68, 77
De Noyelle, Charles Joseph, 66
De Raymond, Charles, 95, 99
Deruisseaux, Paul, 21, 75
Detroit, administrative expense, 32
 agricultural development, 43ff., 54
 commandant, 14
 fur trade, 37
 illegal trade, 59
 Indian problems, 65ff.
 Indian revolt, 86ff.
 population, 37
 trading convoys, 57
De Verchères, Jean Jarret, Sieur, 72, 90
Douville, Alexander Dagneau, Sieur de, 92
Dress of people, 38
Dubuisson, Joseph Guyon, 88, 92
Eau de vie, evils, 21
 tax, 29
Écarlatines, defined, 58
Écrivain principal, office, 15, 16, 17
Education, 19-20
English, complicity in Indian revolt, 94-95
 control of sea and French commerce, 62
 intrigue with western Indians, 87, 96
 King George's War, 33, 79ff.
 trade policies, 51ff.

III

Faux sauniers, 40, 47-48
Finances, Canadian, 28ff.
  charities and religious subsidies, 19, 34
  Chickasaw War, 34
  colonial, 22ff.
  expense of administration, 23, 31
  extraordinary expenses, 23
  King George's War, 32-33
  Louisiana, 25ff.
  system of expenditure, 22ff.
Flour, production in the Illinois, 41ff.
Food of the people, 38
Fur trade, effect of war, 55, 60, 62, 85ff.
  French skill, 51
  furs in demand, 57-58
  liquor traffic, 58-59
  loss to the English at Oswego, 58, 62
  means of exchange, 57
  prices, 58, 61-62
  statistics, 60
  systems of exploitation, 52ff.
Franciscans, 19
Garde magazin, office, 15, 17
Glen, James, 85
Governor, office, 9-11
  friction with intendant, 10-11
Grain prices, 45
Hocquart, Gilles, 10, 11, 28, 58, 68
Houses, construction, 37
Illinois, administration, 12, 14
  agriculture, 40ff.
  annual convoy, 27
  flour exports, 41ff.
  future, 49-50
  Indian unrest, 92ff., 99
  land grants, 40
  lawlessness, 56
  lead mining, 47ff.
  made a part of Louisiana, 25
  religious conditions, 39
Indians, administration, 33, 64-65
  annual conferences, 64-65
  Chickasaw War, 83ff.
  Choctaw revolt, 84-85
  domiciliated tribes, 64
  French policy, 64-65
  Huron, attempted removal from Detroit, 65-69
  King George's War, 79ff.
  Lake of the Two Mountains, settlement, 75-76
  Marin's policy, 70ff.
  Missouri problem, 74-75
  Ottawa discontent at Michilimakinac, 69-70
  presents, 27, 33
  problem of Seneca and others south of the Great Lakes, 77ff.
  Shawnee, removal to the lower Ohio, 66, 76
  southern tribes, 82-83
  western tribes, revolt, 32, 60, 86ff.
Industry, copper mining, 48
  fur trade, 51ff.
  iron foundries at St. Maurice, 30
  lead mining, 47ff.
  salt production, 48
  shipbuilding at Quebec, 30
Intendant, office, 9-11
  friction with governor, 10-11
Jesuits, attitude toward liquor traffic, 22
  college, 18
  influence with savages, 22
  missions, 19, 64
  system of land tenure at Detroit, 44-45
Johnson, Sir William, 51, 59, 81, 97, 98, 99
Justice, organization and administration, 16-17
Kalm, Peter, 13, 20, 28, 37, 38, 39, 45, 46, 49
King George's War, effect on fur trade, 60
  expenditures, 32-33
  part played by western Indians, 78ff.
La Corne Dubreuil, François Josué de, 73
La Demoiselle, Miami chief, 78, 92, 93, 94, 95, 97, 99
La Galissonière, Michel Rolland Barin, Marquis de, 14, 19, 20, 46, 49, 50, 55, 56, 91, 96, 99
Laguin, 77
La Jonquière, Pierre Jacques Taffanel, Marquis de, 64, 99
Land grants, system, 40, 43
La Pérade, Charles François Xavier Tarieu, Sieur de la Pérade, de la Naudière, 89
La Richardie, Armand de, 44, 65, 66, 67, 88
La Ronde, Louis Denys, Sieur de, 48, 49
La Ronde (fils), Louis Denys, Sieur de, 48, 49, 54
La Vérendrye, Pierre Gautier de Varennes, Sieur de, 10, 53, 54, 63, 73, 74, 79, 90
Law, John, 35
Livestock, 45-46
Longueuil, Paul Joseph le Moyne, fourth baron, 43, 71, 86, 87, 88, 89, 90, 92, 93

INDEX

Louisiana, administration, 12
  finances, 23ff.
  health of the people, 39
  posts and settlements, 35-36
  population, 35
  slavery limited, 36
Luc de la Corne, Sieur de St. Luc, 80, 81, 82, 90
Lusignan, Paul Louis Dazenard, Sieur de, 54, 55, 56, 73, 74
Machault, Jean Baptiste Machault d'Arnouville, 46
Marin, Pierre Paul, 70, 71, 72, 73, 74
Mercier, Father Jacques, 84
Michel, Honoré, Sieur de la Rouvillière et Villebois, 28, 46
Michilimakinac, agriculture, 45-46
  Indian problems, 69ff.
  revolt of Indians, 90-91
Military forces, discipline and morale, 13-14
  number and distribution, 12-13
  militia, 12-13
  official appointments, 12
Mingo Puscuss, Choctaw chief, 84
Mining, copper, 48ff.
  lead, 47ff.
  salt, 48
Missions Étrangères, 18, 19
Mississippi Company, 40
Missouri, French establishment, 36, 75
  Indian relations, 74ff.
  liquor trade forbidden, 21
Money and exchange, 22-23, 28
  cards and bills, 22-23
Montchervaux, Jean François Tisserant de, 27, 28
Montreal, distribution of Indian presents, 33
  expenditures for war, 33
  Indian settlements, 64
  jurisdiction, 10-11
  liquor trade restricted, 21
  religious foundations, 18-19, 34
  trading convoys, 57
Navarre, Robert, 77
New England, in King George's War, 80
New Orleans, administrative center, 12
  admiralty jurisdiction, 16
  inferior jurisdiction, 16-17
  population, 35
Nicolas, Huron chief, 65, 87, 89, 91, 92

Notary, office, 17-18
Ohio expedition of Céloron, 97ff.
Ordonnateur, explanation, 12
Oswego, French antagonism, 95-96, 99
  interference with French trade, 54, 58, 62
  spared by French, 80
Ouakantapé, Sioux chief, 72
Pendalouan, Ottawa chief, 69, 70, 90, 91
Pennsylvania, difficulties with liquor trade, 59
  relation to Indian revolt, 94-95
  traders on the Ohio, 92
Piquet, Abbé François, 99
Pontbriand, Henri du Breuil de, Bishop, 20, 21
Post commandant, powers and duties, 14
  qualifications required, 65
Pouchot, 36, 37, 39
Punishment for crime, 17
Quebec, administration, 11-12
  distribution of Indian presents, 33
  expenditures for war, 33
  Indian settlements, 64
  religious foundations, 18-19, 34
  shipbuilding, 30
Recollets, 19, 40
Red Shoe, Choctaw chief, 84, 85
Renault, Philippe François, 47
Sabrevois, Clement Sabrevois de Bleury, 44
St. Clair, Benoist de, 74, 75, 99
St. Pierre, Jacques le Gardeur, Sieur de, 80, 82, 89, 90, 91
Salmon, Edmé Gatien, 16, 24, 25, 26, 47
Sastaredzy, Huron chief, 87, 88
Six Nations, Mohawk in war on the French, 81
  negotiations with French, 79
  Seneca and others, 77ff.
Slaves, importation limited, 36, 40-41
Soeurs de Congregation, 19
Sulpicians, 18, 19, 34, 64
Taychatin, Huron chief, 87, 88
Ursulines, 19
Vaudreuil, Pierre François Rigaud de Cavagnol, Marquis de, 14, 21, 25, 26, 27, 40, 56, 57, 75, 84, 92, 93, 94
Virginia, Ohio land company formed, 96
  traders on the Mississippi, 84
Vivier, Father Louis, 39, 41
Weiser, Conrad, 51, 59, 94, 95